# WALKS IN EAST SUSSEX

## Derek Palmer

## With Historical Notes

**COUNTRYSIDE BOOKS**
NEWBURY, BERKSHIRE

COUNTRYSIDE BOOKS
3 Catherine Road
Newbury, Berkshire


ISBN 1 85306 239 1

Cover photograph of Cuckmere Haven taken by Andy Williams
Sketch maps by Brenda Palmer

Produced through MRM Associates Ltd., Reading
Printed in England by J.W. Arrowsmith Ltd., Bristol

# WALKS IN
# EAST SUSSEX

*Countryside Books' walking guides cover most areas of England
and include the following series:*

*County Rambles*
*Walks for Motorists*
*Exploring Long Distance Paths*
*Literary Walks*
*Pub Walks*

*A complete list is available from the publishers at
3 Catherine Road, Newbury, Berkshire*

# Contents

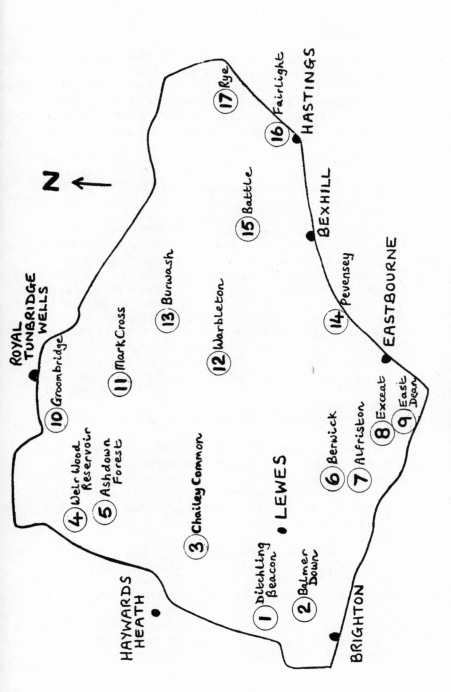

Area map showing the location of the walks.

# Introduction

Even if you are resident in East Sussex it is quite likely you have not explored your county to the full. Some areas chosen for the walks may be worthwhile introductions to places you just happened to notice on signposts as you sped by. Others will be better-known beauty spots you have always intended to visit. So this book is for you as much as it is for the visitor. Everyone should find something of interest.

It was fascinating for me to investigate some of the locations for the first time as well as revisit others I had previously discovered to be excellent walking country. East Sussex is a county of contrasts with its dramatic, mainly clifftop coastline and its famous South Downs hill range descending to the green (and in summer, multi-coloured) patchwork of the Weald. Water is always a pleasant feature on a walk, whether it be the sea, a lake, a river or a myriad of streams. Such features predominate in East Sussex and so are frequently well in view on the walks. One of the country's largest open spaces, Ashdown Forest, is a gift to those who love the great outdoors and desire the opportunity to explore, so naturally it has been included in the book.

Of course, it is possible for anyone with an Ordnance Survey map, and maybe a compass, to find their way around the public footpaths and bridleways, but many of these are not as obvious as they should be. Aided by this book you will discover paths that you may otherwise have experienced difficulty in locating or felt intimidated from using. You will walk with the knowledge that someone has ironed out some of the wrinkles that you might have encountered.

The routes range from a two hour stroll to a 15 mile excursion that may require the best part of a day and they reflect the diversity of the county's many facets. The distance quoted for each walk is approximate, but accurate to within ½ mile. An estimate of actual walking time is given, based on a reasonably good pace, so you should allow extra for stops, and particularly if you are walking as a family.

The routes follow public footpaths, though bear in mind that changes in rights of way do occur from time to time. Remember, too, that it is always advisable to wear a strong pair of walking shoes or boots since you are likely to find the odd patch of mud, even in dry weather.

All of the routes are circular and the starting points have space for car parking nearby. Details of public transport are given where appropriate but you are strongly recommended to check

British Rail timetables as some of the stations mentioned have an infrequent service. Bus routes are, of course, a little more complicated. Services are often even less frequent than the trains and sometimes only run on one day of the week and mostly not at all on Sundays. East Sussex County Council publish bus timetables for certain areas and have available a wide range of others covering the entire county.

Refreshment possibilities are mentioned in an introductory paragraph to each walk. Most country inns welcome walkers, more so if they take the trouble to remove their muddy boots.

Places of particular interest are indicated in the text by the initials HN and further information about them may be found in a special Historical Notes section at the end of each walk.

I dedicate the book to my wife, Brenda, who not only checked all the text with me but also painstakingly drew all the sketch maps. These maps provide a straightforward plan of the route to be followed. The numbers on the diagrams identify the numbered paragraphs in the text and are useful as an aid for checking your position. It is unnecessary to use any other maps, but for those who wish to do so, the numbers for the relevant Ordnance Survey Landranger and Pathfinder maps have been quoted. The grid reference relates to the suggested starting point but it is often possible to start at another point if it happens to be more convenient for access, parking or public transport, etc.

I would like to thank the members of the Downs and Weald Walkers who accompanied me on some of these routes and subsequently helped me re-check them. Their company made the rambles especially enjoyable. I hope that you derive as much pleasure from your outings as we did.

Derek Palmer
spring 1994

To DITCHLING

Ditchling
Beacon

Westmeston
Church

① SOUTH DOWNS WAY

Streathill
Farm

⑤

②

High Park
Farm

④

Highpark
Wood

③

N

To
BRIGHTON

# Ditchling Beacon and High Park Wood

**Introduction:** Starting from one of the South Downs' highest points, this is a particularly appealing walk taking you through some splendid, mature beechwoods. Downland is always at its best when viewed from paths rather than roads and this walk will lead you to fine views and much that is hidden from those not prepared to explore on foot. If you happen to be of a nervous disposition and walking in May, see historical note for Westmeston.

**Distance:** At 5½ miles this is one of our shortest walks and, without rushing, will be completed in 2–2½ hours.

**Refreshments:** On all summer days, and most weekends too out of season, you will find an ice cream van in the car park. There are two good pubs serving hot and cold food lunchtimes and evenings in Ditchling village.

**How to get there:** From the village of Ditchling travel for 1½ miles southwards up the winding road to the free National Trust car park on top of Ditchling Beacon. There is a bus service to Ditchling from Lewes and Burgess Hill Mondays to Fridays and from Brighton on Fridays only. OS maps 198 or 1288 (TQ 21/31), grid reference TQ 333130.

**The Walk**
**1.** From the car park pass the information board and go over a stile beyond it. Head in a westerly direction along the South Downs Way and reach another information board. Turn left over a stile and follow the path over a field. Go through a gate and continue, at first with a wire fence on your left, later between fences. Pass a turning on the left and start to descend. At the bottom of the slope go through a gate and bear left, then right round the hillside following the fence on your left. You reach a gate and turn left up to a road.

**2.** Cross the road, half right, to a footpath and shortly reach a post where you bear left passing a barn on your left. Ignore a right turn and continue ahead. The buildings of High Park Farm come into view on your left and you go over a crossing track and bear right where a track from the farmyard comes in from the left. On a clear day the sea should be in view over to your right. As you start to descend, a flint wall is over to your left. In another ½ mile you reach a crossing track under power cables.

**3.** Turn sharp left downhill on a very attractive, woodland path and at the bottom of the slope reach a gate in the valley. Make your way along the left side of a field and come to another gate. Continue with an arable field on your left and a sloping, uncultivated field on your right. Later you commence ascending towards a gate. Go over a crossing track and bear slightly left across a field, then diagonally right across the next field and reach a stile by a farm gate.

**4.** Turn left along a farm track later entering the farmyard. Just before you reach a bungalow turn right over a stile and then turn left on another farm track maintaining your original direction. Go past the buildings of Streathill Farm and reach a bridle gate.

**5.** Turn left over the tarred farm driveway and through another bridle gate. Continue on the fine ridge path forming part of the South Downs Way for 1¼ miles back to the car park. Very shortly the hamlet of Westmeston (HN) comes into view down to your right. The village of Ditchling (HN) lies beyond to the north west.

**Historical Notes**

**Ditchling Beacon,** at 800 ft, is the second highest point on the South Downs and the highest in Sussex. The area is protected by The National Trust. It was an important link in the chain of beacon hills where huge fires were lit to signal the imminent arrival of the Spanish Armada. On the horizon to the north you can see the North Downs. To the south east you may spot the chalk bulk of Seaford Head behind Newhaven harbour. The mound to the west is Wolstonbury Hill near Pyecombe and in view to the south west is Chanctonbury Ring and, nearer, the famous beauty spot of Devil's Dyke.

**Westmeston** and the surrounding area abound with ghost stories. On a windy day, from 24th–26th May listen for the sound of phantom horses' hooves and moaning men fleeing from battle. You may also catch a nasty smell.

The church has a 17th century porch, incorporating 14th century timbers, and a shingled bell turret. Westmeston Place has some fine perpendicular-style windows dating from around 1500. The house is said to be haunted by a monk who carves at a panel.

Between Westmeston and Ditchling is Black Dog Hill where the unlucky may hear the whines of a headless black dog killed by a gamekeeper.

**Ditchling** is well worth exploring as part of your day out. Opposite the church is Wing Place, previously called The Royal Palace. It has to be at least 500 years old and is said to have been presented to Anne of Cleves by King Henry VIII. Some have claimed it was built by King Alfred the Great and that it is described in the Domesday Book. Other personalities who more recently have been drawn to the village are the actress Ellen Terry, cartoonist Rowland Emmett and World War II Forces' Sweetheart, Dame Vera Lynn.

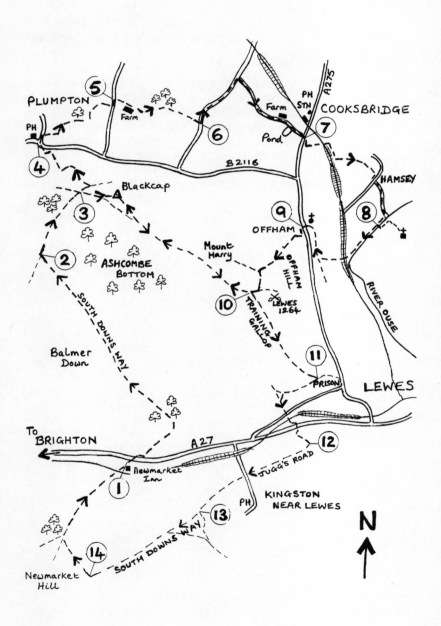

# Lewes, Blackcap and Balmer Down

**Introduction:** Besides following part of the much-walked South Downs Way (SDW) you will also be discovering many little-used paths along the route. There is a variety of scenery and, on a clear day, the views are memorable. The countryside around the fascinating county town of Lewes is steeped in history. As you travel along the tracks, the main highways of the past, try imagining the massive battles which took place on these hills all of 700 years ago.

**Distance:** Taken in its entirety of 15 miles, this walk represents a fairly energetic, all-day ramble but it may be split instead into two separate walks of 10 and 8 miles, taking around 4 and 3½ hours respectively.

**Refreshments:** There are public houses strategically dotted around the route and, irrespective of where you start or finish, there is a pub. The first is The Newmarket Inn on the A27 near Falmer which has plenty of choice. The Half Moon at Plumpton is quite accustomed to walkers calling and has an interesting menu, and The Pump House in Cooksbridge makes a useful stop. The Juggs Arms at Kingston, as with all the others, offers food seven days a week. If you are stopping off in Lewes you have all the variety of hotels, pubs, tea shops, cafes and shops that you would expect a county town to offer, and the closest public house, just off the route, is The Windmill. It is quite small but offers hot lunches and the landlord does not blanch at the sight of muddy boots.

**How to get there:** The 15 mile walk may be commenced from one of the following places:

The Newmarket Inn on the A27 (point 1 – grid reference TQ 378092), where there is a layby for parking 100 yards west of the inn.

The Half Moon at Plumpton (point 4 – grid reference TQ 364133). There is limited parking in the village but, with permission, and if you are intending to visit it, you may be able to use the large car park at the rear of the pub.

Cooksbridge railway station (point 7 – grid reference TQ 401134) where there is parking space off the A275 opposite Hamsey Lane, about 200 yards north of the station.

Behind Lewes Prison (point 11 – grid reference TQ 403101) from where the railway station is about ½ mile distant. There are plenty of car parks in the town. Make for the prison and join a track behind it.

The 10 mile walk may be commenced from The Newmarket Inn or from Lewes Prison.

The 8 mile walk may be commenced from Plumpton or Cooksbridge.

If public transport is required the best option would be to commence the walk from Lewes where trains and buses run from Brighton, Haywards Heath, Seaford and Eastbourne. OS maps 198 or 1307 (TQ 20/30, 1288 (TQ 21/31), 1289 (TQ 41/51), and 1308 (TQ 40/50 – very small part only).

**The Walk**
**1.** From the parking area just beyond The Newmarket Inn return to the filling station and cross the main road. Turn right to the South Downs Way (HN) signpost. Go up a slope to a bridle gate and continue uphill. You reach a flint wall and take the choice of stile or bridle gate to go through some woodland. The next bridle gate leads you out of the woods onto rolling downland. You go downhill to a stile and then up again between fields to a metal bridle gate. Continue along the left side of a field going steadily uphill on Balmer Down. As the path levels out you should see a dew pond on your right – what was originally a natural phenomenon has been 'improved' by man with some cement! The field switches between pasture and arable and gates on right and left indicate the existence of a crossing bridleway. You continue towards power lines and the hill crest ahead to reach a T junction.
**2.** Turn right on an enclosed bridleway, still following the direction of the SDW. For about ½ mile there is no possibility of losing your way and, soon after passing some woodland on your left, you reach a crossing track beyond which is a farm gate and you turn right through a bridle gate. **For the full walk continue from point 3.**

**For the 10 mile walk continue as follows:** Once through the bridle gate continue right, alongside a fence, soon bearing left at a fork, away from the fence up to the triangulation point on Blackcap. Continue downhill to rejoin the fence and shortly go through a bridle gate. Maintain direction and later go through another bridle gate by a pylon. The large buildings ahead to your right are racing stables. Later you ignore a right fork leading to them and continue ahead for another 150 yards and take a turning on the right. **Proceed from point 10.**

**3.** Continue along with a small slope on your left and soon your path bears right, downhill to a junction of paths. Here you turn sharply left and go fairly steeply downhill. Go through a gate and later ignore an inviting right turn. Ignore also a left turning into a disused quarry. Only a few yards beyond this look to your left for an easily-missed path through some trees leading to a stile. Bear diagonally right across a field to another stile and maintain direction across the next field to a stile leading out to a road. Do not join the road but turn left onto a parallel path for a while until you are led onto the road and into the village of Plumpton (HN).

**4.** The Half Moon Inn (HN) is ahead but you need to turn right up Plumpton Lane for 100 yards or so where you turn right over a stile. Cross a small field and go over another stile, then over a crossing track into a field. You soon turn left and then bear diagonally right towards the corner of some woods. Turn right along the edge of the wood, later turning left and, after going over the drive to a house, bear diagonally right across a field passing a clump of trees on your left. Via two stiles you go over a crossing track and along the left side of a field making for some barns ahead. When you reach a lane turn left.

**5.** In a few yards turn right on a farm track. Pass the farm buildings on your right and leave the farm track by going through a bridle gate into a field. You are led towards another bridle gate where you bear diagonally left to the next bridle gate leading into some woods. This woodland path will be very muddy after rain. As you reach a more open area be ready to turn right to leave the woods and go under power lines towards a copse. Bear left and then right to cross a large field towards barns and arrive at a tarred lane.

**6.** Turn left along the lane passing a pond on your left and in about ½ mile you come to a road junction. Turn right on the road which is signposted to Cooksbridge. You pass Lower Tulleywells Farm on your left and reach a lake on your right. (If you require either Cooksbridge railway station or The Pump House pub turn left. Follow the direction of the public footpath sign across a field to a stile and turn right to go along the side of the railway.) Continue down the road to the main A275 at Cooksbridge (HN).

**7.** Cross the road and turn right for a few yards looking out for a yellow waymark on a telegraph pole. If you find you are passing the village hall called The Malthouse (HN), you have missed the waymark. Turn left on a private driveway to a house, soon going through a gate on the left leading you onto an enclosed path and over a stile. Go over a small meadow, then over another stile and a bridge over a ditch. The next stile leads you to the railway line which you should cross with care. Immediately turn right alongside a field to another stile in the corner. Maintain direction along the next field to cross yet another stile. Turn left away from the railway and go down to the bottom of a field and then over a stile. Maintain direction across the next field, which may be in crop, past some sheds on your immediate right and out to a lane. Turn right for a few yards and then left down another lane and continue into the hamlet of Hamsey. You pass a farm on your right and reach the bank of the river Ouse. Turn right along the bank to reach a bridge.

**8.** (A short diversion will take you to see the remote Hamsey church (HN) if you cross the bridge and follow the lane to it, later retracing your steps.) Keep alongside the river bank for ½ mile and go under a railway bridge. Go ahead to reach a T junction and turn right with woods on your left. You reach Offham church and bear left along a lane to the main road at Offham (HN).

**9.** Cross the road (The Blacksmiths Arms is to your right) and turn left for a short distance then turn right onto the bridleway leading to Blackcap. Soon ignore a little path leading to a stile on your left. Continue on the main track past a barn and steadily climb Offham Hill (HN) for about ½ mile. As the path starts to level out ignore a left turn and immediately after an isolated group of shrubs turn left on a wide, grassy path between fields. At a T junction turn right for about 100 yards to reach a turning on the left. **For the full walk continue from point 10.**

For the 8 mile walk continue as follows: Go ahead on the main, chalky track for about ½ mile. Ignore a left fork, continuing under power lines and going through a couple of bridle gates. A track joins you from the right and you bear away from the fence on your left towards a post and the triangulation point on Blackcap. Make your way downhill to reach a crossing track with a farm gate and bridle gate. You go through neither but turn right and **proceed from point 3.**

**10.** Turn left, shortly going over a tarred drive leading to racing stables and keep on the main track with a training gallop over on your right. The sprawl of Lewes is well in evidence on your left and, on a clear day, the sea should be visible way ahead. Later your track bears left and you reach a junction with the sinister wall of Lewes Prison, built in 1853, in front of you. (If you wish to visit the historic town of Lewes (HN) with its many attractions, turn left and you will soon arrive in the town centre. Retrace your steps to rejoin the walk.)

**11.** Turn sharp right passing the end of the gallop that you previously walked alongside. You pass the backs of houses and later, 100 yards or so beyond the last fence, you should look for a narrow, chalky, winding, downhill path through shrubs. This leads out to a main track by a farm entrance. Turn left and reach a main road which you cross to join a bridleway opposite, soon going under a railway bridge. Bear left to a footbridge taking you over the main A27. Go through a bridle gate and another gate and continue uphill across a field to the next bridle gate and out to a track.

**12.** Turn right along this track (Jugg's Road) and in a ½ mile or so you cross over a road in the village of Kingston (HN). (Turn left here along the road for about 1/3 mile for The Juggs Arms (HN). Retrace your steps to rejoin the walk.) Maintain direction along a residential road where, if walking too quickly, you may be in danger of tripping over the speed-reducing ramps! The road bears to the right but you continue ahead on an enclosed track and, after going through a gate, reach a fork.

**13.** Keep right, climbing steeply uphill, and in ¼ mile you go over a stile and rejoin the South Downs Way. Continue ahead, firstly close to the fence on your right and later bearing away from it to reach a gate with Newmarket Hill (HN) beyond.

**14.** Continue following the SDW by bearing right along a field edge. A bridle gate leads you down the edge of the next field towards a plantation. At a metal gate there is a junction of paths where you bear right on a wide, grassy track going downhill. On a clear day you will have a wonderful, panoramic view of most of the area in which you have just walked. Go through a farm gate and along the left edge of the next field. You reach your last gate, pass some houses, go under the railway and come out to the A27, turning left to the car parking area.


**Historical Notes**

**The South Downs Way** is one of Britain's most clearly waymarked and well-maintained long distance footpaths, ideal for day trips because of easy access to short sections gained from many trunk roads cutting across it. It is also the only long distance bridleway, so expect to see horseriders and mountain bikers.

**Plumpton** was the home of Old Martha, a 19th century eccentric, claimed by locals to be a witch. She lived to be 100 and, although supposedly rich, dressed in wild attire and tramped miles of countryside singing and dancing as she went along ringing little bells. The only known photograph of her was one taken surreptitiously from behind a bush. John Dudeney's (see Newmarket Hill below) childhood home has been identified as The Cottage, across the road from The Half Moon.

**The Half Moon** has an unusual feature in the bar – a painting of more than 100 of the pub's regulars. A Sussex portrait painter, Dick Leech, was commissioned by the pub's landlord to undertake the huge montage over a period of nine months in 1979.

**Cooksbridge** has been world famous for orchids for over a century. A Scotsman, James Ure McBean, moved into the village in 1875, bought some land and erected greenhouses. McBean Orchids has proliferated into a business which has won hundreds of prizes for its new varieties. The village's original claim to fame was in 1264 when Simon de Montfort's infantrymen stopped here on their way to the Battle of Lewes for breakfast served by 'cooks on the bridge'.

**The Malthouse** is owned by Lord Monk Bretton but it is used as the village hall at a peppercorn rent of 1/- per year (not 5p but a good old bob!)

**Hamsey church** is on a curious island site, once a fortified settlement complete with manor house and medieval church. This is definitely something from a less enlightened age and the serfs must have been held in terror as they passed the peering gargoyles. There is a belief that the hamlet was wiped out by plague and the survivors chose to perish rather than spread the disease from their island site.

**Offham**, pronounced 'Oaf-ham', is the site of an early piece of railway engineering, in the early 19th century when chalk and lime mines and quarries were at their peak. The mine here was a steep 400 ft above the transportation facility on the river Ouse below, a treacherous descent for the traditional horse and cart method. The mine owner, George Shiffner, commissioned William Jessop to design and build one of the county's first 'railways'. The empty waggons, connected to cables, were hauled to the top by the weight of the full ones travelling down, via tunnels under the road, to the waiting barges below. Turntables at top and bottom of the slope were part of the innovative approach to the problem.

**Offham Hill** is the site of the Battle of Lewes fought with great ferocity on 14 May, 1264. Forces commanded by Simon de Montfort took the high ground and defeated those of Henry III ensconced in the town of Lewes below.

**Lewes** is the county town of East Sussex and is steeped in history. Its name is thought to be accounted for by its hilltop position, the Old English 'hlaew' meaning hill. The Saxons used this steep spur on the South Downs as a fortified stronghold but centuries earlier the Romans were here and before their arrival there was an Iron Age hillfort.

**Kingston**, with its tidy line of flint cottages and smart houses leading up to the Downs, has a genteel appearance today. In Ashcombe Lane is the grave of Nan Kemp, who was hanged after murdering her baby and serving the wretched infant in a pie to her husband. Macabre legends and sightings of her 'ghost' have been part of village mythology ever since.

**Jugg's Road** was once a thoroughfare linking Lewes with Brighton. The name of the village inn, The Juggs Arms, immortalises the road, and the decorous fishwives, who used it to bring their husband's catches from the sea, are commemorated on the pub sign.

**Newmarket Hill** was thoroughly walked 200 years ago by one of the county's most interesting characters. He was John Dudeney, a shepherd who was also a scholar. Whilst tending the sheep, although without formal schooling, he taught himself to read the Bible in its original Hebrew. Eventually he was able to descend from the hill for good, becoming one of Lewes's best-respected school teachers who was also instrumental in the establishment of the town's Mechanics Institute.

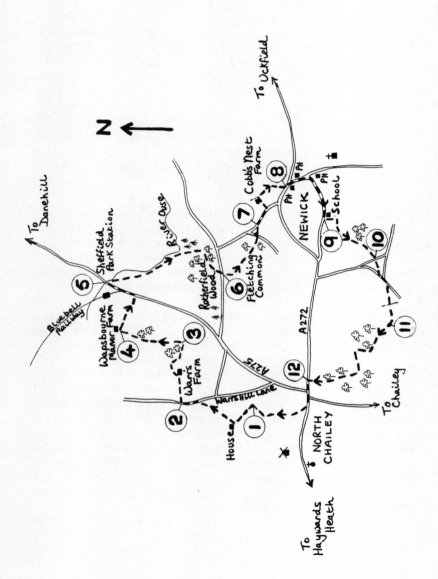

# Newick and Chailey Common

**Introduction:** This walk is easy to follow and although crossing fairly flat terrain you will have some excellent views at many points. It commences on the Chailey Common Nature Reserve and takes you along a short stretch of the river Ouse. There may be an opportunity to take a ride on the Bluebell Railway and you can explore the village of Newick.

**Distance:** This approximately 7½ mile circuit will take around 3½–4 hours if walked at a reasonably steady pace.

**Refreshments:** Three of Newick's public houses are passed, as is the village shop which sells confectionery, drinks and ice cream. The Bull's Head offers hot and cold food lunchtimes and evenings. Also, part way round the walk you have the Bessemer Arms on Sheffield Park station which offers refreshments and snacks. It is open for much of the day even when the Bluebell Line is not operating.

**How to get there:** The walk commences from the Chailey Common car park in Warrs Hill Lane off the A275, north of North Chailey village. If more convenient it may be commenced from the village green at Newick (point 8), on the A272, where there is limited parking. Buses run to Newick from Lewes on Mondays to Saturdays. OS maps 198 or 1268 (TQ 22/32) and 1269 (TQ 42/52), grid references TQ 392218 (Chailey Common) or TQ 418214 (Newick).

**The Walk**
**1.** Leave the Chailey Common (HN) car park at the far end and, passing a signboard on your right, continue in a westerly direction. (You should be able to see a windmill ahead, slightly left.) In 100 yards or so bear right and, keeping to the main track, continue along the hillside. (There is a myriad of paths here so if you should misinterpret the following instructions do not worry – just use the

house at the bottom of the slope as your objective.) In another 150 yards fork right downhill. In about another 100 yards your path widens and you turn right onto a narrower one. You should be walking parallel to a marshy dip on your immediate right. In about another 100 yards turn right and, at the bottom of the slope, bear right to go over a sleeper bridge and soon over another. At the ensuing fork go left and then through a gap in the fence by the house for which you were aiming. Turn right along the pink driveway and onto a tarred one. Turn right and, immediately, left into woods towards some houses which you pass on your left. Continue on a tarred driveway and reach a fingerpost leading you into more woods. Go through a squeeze stile near a gate, then another, over a plank bridge and, after passing an electricity pylon, out to a road. Turn left and shortly reach the entrance to Warrs Farm.

**2.** Turn right along the farm drive and when you reach the farmhouse turn left through double gates and immediately right through another gate. Shortly go through a gateway on your right into a field. Follow the right of way diagonally right across the field but if this is ploughed over or in crop you may prefer to continue with the following instructions in parentheses. (Go along the left side of the field and at the bottom turn right, with woods on your left, and reach the second of two metal gates.) Turn left into the woods (waymark on tree) soon going over a bridge and reach an open area where you go under electricity cables into more woods. Bear right to follow the direction of a couple of waymarks on trees and go through a gate into a field.

**3.** Turn left along the side of the field. Go under the cables you passed earlier and when the woods end continue ahead over a large, rough field crossing towards the woodland on the right. Go through the fence ahead at a waymark and proceed on a wide, tree-lined track. Once over a bridge enter a farmyard with many caravans (these are used by strawberry pickers) and reach a T junction at Wapsbourne Manor Farm.

**4.** Turn right on a roadway and follow this, left and right past the ancient farmhouse and come out to a road. Turn left and shortly enter Sheffield Park (HN). You soon reach the end of the Bluebell Line (HN) at Sheffield Park station. (Besides the possibility of your taking a ride on the railway there are refreshment and toilet facilities here.)

**5.** By the Bluebell Railway sign turn right down a bank and go over a stile. Bear slightly right across a field making for a point where overhead telephone wires cross the bank of the river Ouse. Cross a stile by a gate and continue with the river on your left and later go down some steps and over a ford. Cross a metal barrier into Rotherfield Wood and, after going under power cables, you will reach a wide, grassy crossing track. Turn right and, just after passing a left fork, you will reach a road.

**6.** Cross the road to the stony track opposite and soon pass some very large greenhouses on your right. Immediately after passing some buildings turn left, go through a metal gate, across a field and over a stile. Continue over two more stiles and into an area of woodland on Fletching Common. Your path meanders through the woods and, after going over a stile by a gate, you come out to a road. Turn left up the road for about 50 yards and opposite a wooden barrier turn right into an area of bracken and trees. Soon fork left, join a path coming in from the left and then turn left. There are several little paths here but if you keep in a north-easterly direction for a 100 yards or so you will reach another road.

**7.** Turn right along the road and soon go over a stream. The road starts to ascend and, in about another 200 yards, next to the entrance to Cobb's Nest Farm, turn left on an enclosed path. At a T junction turn right and reach a small housing estate. Continue ahead on a road and opposite the second turning on the right turn left on an enclosed, tarred path. Pass some houses and continue ahead along a lane which brings you out to the village green at Newick (HN).

**8.** Cross the main A272 road to The Bull Inn and bear left on a road to pass The Royal Oak. Later another pub, The Crown, comes into view but before reaching it you turn right into Allington Road. Go past the post office and after passing a school you will find a concrete public footpath sign.

**9.** Turn left on an enclosed path and go over a stile by a wooden public footpath sign. Turn right along the side of a field, later cutting its corner towards a gate. Do not go through the gate but continue down the field and in its corner go over a stile into another field. Cross it diagonally right to go over another stile, then across a bridge and straight ahead past some woods managed by the Woodland Trust on your left. You come to a superfluous stile and bear right up a slope and over the next stile. Continue on a driveway, passing a house on your right and reach a lane.

**10.** Cross over to the enclosed path opposite and shortly reach a road. Turn left and pass a left turning and, in about 150 yards, bear right over a stile. Head across a field between two oak trees to a solitary oak and over a stile beyond. Go over a crossing track and continue straight ahead on a path which affords good views over to your left. Go over a stile then straight across a garden and out through a gate.

**11.** Turn right for a few yards and then left over a stile. Bear diagonally right across a field and, a little to your left, the spire of Chailey church comes into view. Once over the next stile you go straight ahead on a fenced track. Shortly you will be passing woodland over on your right. Your track bears right and, at a fork, keep left downhill. After passing a gate turn left, following a stream down on your right which you shortly cross via a sleeper bridge. Bear right over another and then over a crossing track to a stile which you cross to continue through an area of heathland. Go over another stile by a barrier and over a crossing track. Ignoring a right fork, soon go over a stile and along the left side of a field. Go over a stile, cross a residential road and come out to the main A272.

**12.** Cross the road, turn left and soon cross over the A275, passing a filling station over on your left. In another 100 yards bear right onto a public footpath into woods. Shortly continue across an open area of bracken towards a house. (There is a good view of the windmill over on your left.) At a T junction turn left and then immediately right, passing houses on your right. At a junction of paths continue ahead over a sleeper bridge and shortly you will find the car park over on your right.

**Historical Notes**

**Chailey** derives its name from the Anglo-Saxon 'chag' meaning gorse and 'legh' meaning field. The North Common on which you commence your walk (there is another on the southern side of the A272) has been a nature reserve since 1966 and is a SSSI (Site of Special Scientific Interest). It is the centre of all Sussex: East and West; the exact spot is claimed to be the windmill, Beard's Mill (which you will see in the distance). One plant that flourished on the common was bogbean, claimed by locals to be a rheumatism preventative. Other wild plants of medicinal value that were gathered in the past, particularly by gypsies, were honeysuckle berries as a cure for sore throats and young broom shoots as a remedy for kidney infections.

**Sheffield Park** has two claims to fame – firstly the station on the Bluebell Line, and also the park itself. Sheffield Park Garden consists of 100 acres of mature trees and rare shrubs with five lakes. The original landscape design was laid out in the 18th century for Lord Sheffield by 'Capability' Brown. The National Trust bought the gardens in 1954. They are well worth a visit at any time of the year but the leaf cover in autumn is unforgettable.

**The Bluebell Line** was started in 1959 by a group of enthusiasts and has grown over the years to what you see today. This has been achieved through the dedication of mainly volunteer staff. In 1992 an additional mile of line was opened up and the ultimate objective is to link the line to British Rail at East Grinstead. This will include the restoration of a tunnel which will be the longest on a volunteer-run railway. Trains run on the line to Horsted Keynes on Sundays throughout the year and on many Saturdays and weekdays (phone for details (24 hours) – 082 572 2370).

**Newick**, clustering around the triangular village green, copes well with its unfortunate dissection by the busy A272. Standing on a dais-like plinth, the village pump is still in working order and dates from 1837, the year in which Victoria came to the throne. If you take time out of your walk to visit the church you will find a perfect Jacobean pulpit with back and sounding board. Two of the chancel windows have an Agnus Dei in stained glass from the early 14th century.

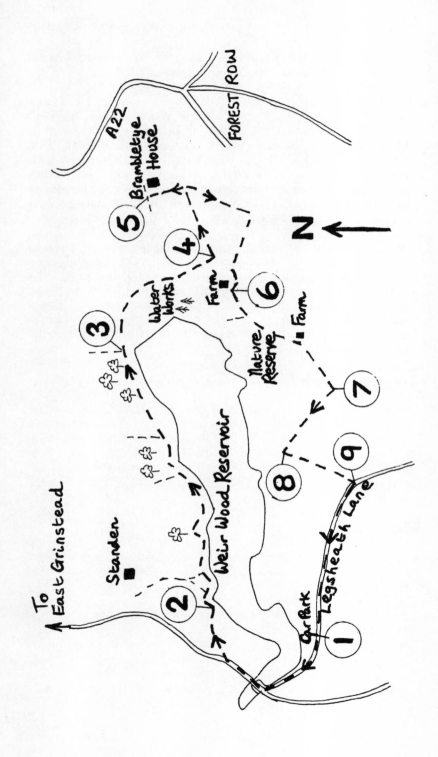

# Weir Wood Reservoir

**Introduction:** This is an easy walk, requiring very little effort over the few gentle slopes. It commences in East Sussex but, for a mile or two, takes you over the border into West Sussex and back again. Besides circumventing the 2-mile long Weir Wood Reservoir you are taken to the ruined, but still evocative, Brambletye House near Forest Row. A short diversion is possible to visit Standen, owned by The National Trust.

**Distance:** The 6½ mile circuit is mainly level and will take around 2½–3 hours to complete.

**Refreshments:** There are no refreshment possibilities on the walk so it may be sensible to take something to drink. The constant sight of so much water could bring on a thirst!

**How to get there:** The car park is in Legsheath Lane, on the southern side of Weir Wood Reservoir. East Grinstead is a couple of miles to the north. On Mondays to Saturdays buses run from Lewes and East Grinstead along the A22 via nearby Forest Row from where the walk may be joined between points 5 and 6. OS maps 187 or 1247 (TQ 23/33) and 1248 (TQ 43/53), grid reference TQ 384341.

**The Walk**
1. From the car park return to the road and turn right. In about ¼ mile reach a junction where you turn right with the reservoir on your right and a small lake on the left. Continue on the road for another ¼ mile and take a turning on the right. Pass a car park and later go through a gate.
2. Turn left and follow the fence on your right, later joining the Sussex Border Path (SBP) which comes in from your left. The next left turning leads to Standen (HN) and you may wish to take a diversion. Otherwise your route continues ahead. Go over a couple of stiles and pass another left turn with two more stiles. The next stile is followed by a plank bridge and you then turn sharply right

with the fence. You reach another signpost and continue ahead, leaving the SBP at an electricity pylon. Power cables that were previously on your left now cross and then re-cross the path. Later a stile leads you into an open area.

**3.** Bear right and you will see the waterworks on the other side of the reservoir. Later pass alongside the waterworks and go over a stile by a rusty pylon and continue ahead to a footbridge. Pass a house and the next stile leads you onto an enclosed path and out to a road. Continue for about another 200 yards and reach a stile.

**4.** Turn left over the stile and go across a field to a public footpath sign and a footbridge. Bear left across a field to a gate and a crossing track where you turn left. Soon go over a bridge and reach the ruins of Brambletye House (HN) and a T junction.

**5.** Turn around and retrace your steps back over the bridge and past the track on the right that you used earlier. In another ⅓ mile you come out to a lane and turn right. After going over a bridge, fork left in the direction of South Park Farm. Pass a right turn and reach the farmhouse and buildings on your right.

**6.** Bear left on a concreted road and pass another house and right turn. Pass by a nature reserve on your right and another house on the left and reach a farmyard. Bear slightly right on the farm track towards a black barn and as you reach it turn right over a stile. Climb a sloping field to another stile. Bear right across the next field to a stile and then bear left across the corner of a third field to reach a gate at the bottom.

**7.** Do not go through the gate but turn right to follow the field boundary round to another gate, which you pass through, heading straight across the next field to a third gate. You should have a good view of the reservoir on your right and there are woods on the left.

**8.** Once through the gate turn left through another. Shortly enter some woods and leave them through a kissing gate. Now bear diagonally right across a sloping field towards some houses. Pass these on your right and use a stile on the right to take you out to the road.

**9.** Turn right along the road for about ¾ mile to reach the car park.

**Historical Notes**

**Weir Wood Reservoir** was completed in 1954, a joint venture of surrounding local authorities. At the western end of the reservoir is the 41 ft high and 1,680 ft long dam. The base is an incredible

300 ft in width. It took about 20,000 cubic yards of concrete to form the cut-off trench alone which was constructed to prevent seepage under the dam. When the valley was flooded two roads were lost along with Admiral's Bridge which has been known to reappear at times of drought.

The reservoir, which spreads over 280 acres and holds over 1,200 million gallons when full, serves nearby East Grinstead and provides a third of its water to Crawley seven miles away. Obviously such a large stretch of water is a mecca for recreational activity, including yachting and angling. It also attracts ornithologists from near and far.

**Standen** is a family house in the care of The National Trust and well worth a visit. It was designed by Philip Webb, a friend of William Morris. The remarkably complete interior has been carefully restored. It contains Morris textiles and wallpapers as well as its original electric light fittings. There is a fine view from its beautiful hillside garden across the Medway valley.

**Brambletye House**, built by Sir Henry Compton in 1631, is a fine example of the Jacobean-Gothic style and, although in ruins, evokes a great sense of history. It featured prominently during the time of the Civil War and Horace Smith later wrote a novel based on its association with the period. Sir James Richards who had earned his 'gong' for his successful commands at sea was the next occupant of the manor, from 1683. He fell foul of King Charles II and was suspected of treason, and the house was raided leading to the discovery of a vast arsenal of arms and ammunition. Sir James fled to his wife's former home in Spain and during the following century the house fell into decay and was partially demolished for use as building material.

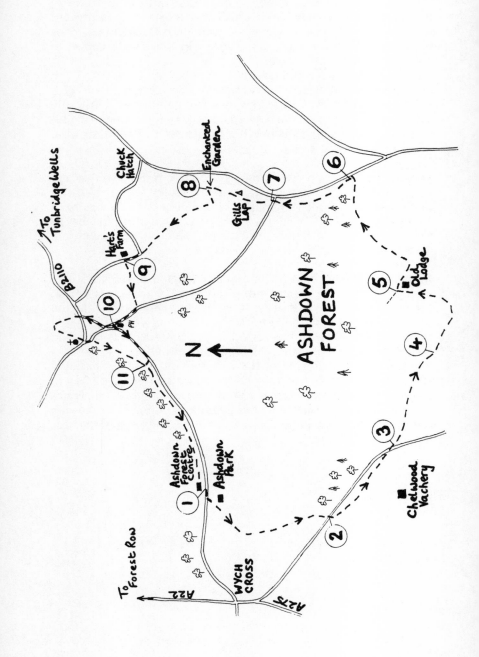

# Ashdown Forest

**Introduction:** The walk explores a small part of the largest area of open space in south east England. This is one of the more energetic walks, perfect for those seeking some exercise and solitude. For much of the route the peace and quiet of the countryside remains undisturbed and there is a strong sense of being at one with nature. As the large number of car parks testify, it is an area that draws a lot of visitors but the route will introduce you to parts that are rarely trod by the great majority.

**Distance:** If you complete the full circuit of 10 miles you should allow for 4½–5 hours of walking. Towards the end it is possible to reduce the length of the walk by almost a mile.

**Refreshments:** A little over 2 miles from the end of the walk you will pass The Hatch Inn at Colman's Hatch where you can obtain hot and cold food lunchtimes and evenings. If your boots are not too muddy use the middle door as the floor in front of the bar here is uncarpeted. Otherwise their removal will be appreciated by the landlady. Confectionery is available at the village shop/post office.

**How to get there:** Leave the A22 at Wych Cross, south of Forest Row, travelling eastwards on the road to Colman's Hatch. In a little less than a mile you will find the Ashdown Forest Centre and car park on your left. Buses run from Uckfield and East Grinstead to the Forest Centre, and to nearby Wych Cross from Haywards Heath and East Grinstead. OS maps 187 and 188 or 1248 (TQ 43/53) and 1269 (TQ 42/52), grid reference TQ 432324.

**The Walk**
1. From the car park return to the road and turn right past the Ashdown Forest Centre (well worth a visit as there is much here describing the history, archaeology, flora and fauna) for about 100 yards as far as a turning on the right. Cross the road to a stile and then follow the direction of a series of fingerposts through the grounds of Ashdown Park (HN). Close to the house bear right on

a track which later becomes raised. After going through a gate you bear right on a well-defined track which eventually takes you over a stile by a gate. Bear slightly right across a field and go through a fence continuing with a ditch on your right. Another stile by a gate leads you through an area of shrubs on a path that will be muddy after rain. Go through a yard with an assortment of vehicles and arrive at the main A22 road.

2. Cross the road (with care!) to a small path opposite which will lead you down to a wide track on which turn left. In a few yards turn right, then almost immediately left on a wide track. When the track forks bear left uphill. You are led over a tarmac drive leading to Chelwood Vachery Residential Training Centre (HN), the large building that you may have noticed over on your right. Shortly go over a crossing track and then maintain direction on a narrow path, crossing a very wide track. You are led back to the A22 by a small car park. Turn right for a few yards and then cross the main road to a larger car park by the entrance to Pippingford. You will find a narrow path on the left by an AA telephone box.

3. Follow the narrow path and continue in a south-easterly direction close to a bank and later you will find a fence (sometimes the remains of one) on your left. The path meanders, often round fallen trees, but the fence is your guide and this leads you to an unusual metal squeeze stile/gate taking you into a conservation area. Please ensure that you secure the gate, then maintain direction and later you will leave the area through another of these gates and, very shortly, the fence reaches a corner.

4. Go ahead over a ditch and soon turn left onto a footbridge over a stream. Turn right and shortly you will reach a T junction (there is a gate a few yards over to your right). Turn left on this well-defined track, later ignoring a right fork. You reach an open area and a wide track but you bear slightly left remaining on the narrow one. You will soon be able to discern the stream again down in the valley on your left. Ignore a right fork and go down to a bridle gate and across a footbridge. Continue on a narrow footpath and later pass a yellow waymark on a tree, now with fields on your right. Soon a large house (Old Lodge) comes into view over on the right and footpath signs lead you to a T junction.

5. Turn right past Old Lodge (HN), continue on the curving, tarred drive for about a mile, passing the lodge houses, and go through a gate to reach a road.

6. Turn left through a barrier and continue on a path which runs parallel to the road. Cross a car park, passing a seat and sign on your immediate left and, keeping to the main path, reach another car park. Bear left to a stone plinth with a plaque indicating

mileages to points in all directions. Bear slightly right on a narrow path leading you back towards the road and follow it to a road junction. Cross over the road to another car park.

**7.** Go over the car park to a wide track running parallel to the road over on your right. You pass a series of seats, useful for those who wish to sit and admire the views, and the triangulation point at Gills Lap (669 ft) over on your right. The track starts to descend and you pass a pond on your right. Just before the track dips turn left and shortly arrive at the entrance to The Enchanted Garden (HN) which you will want to visit.

**8.** Leave the garden via two posts and turn right down to a wide track. Turn left and in about 150 yards look for a narrow path on your right which leads you, in about another 100 yards, to a fork where you branch left onto an even narrower path. Bear slightly left over a wide crossing track and continue steadily downhill, later going through woodland. Ignore little tracks forking left and right and when your main track turns right leave it and continue straight ahead. Go down a steepish slope, pass a deep gully over on your right, and reach a white house which you pass on your left continuing on a gravelled drive. Come out to a lane, turn left and then immediately right along another. The lane bears left and later you reach a road junction. Turn left to cross a bridge over a stream and in a couple of hundred yards reach Hart's Farm on your right.

**9.** Turn left up some stone steps and go through a kissing gate. Continue along the left side of two fields, through another kissing gate, and straight over the next field. You reach a road on which you turn right and proceed uphill with care to find yourself at the, quite probably welcome, Hatch Inn (HN) with a road junction beyond. **If you are doing the whole walk continue from point 10.**

**For the shorter route continue as follows:** At the road junction turn sharp left along the road passing the pub on your left and continue (with care) for ¼ mile as far as the drive, on the left, to The Ridge (and other houses). Turn right on a farm track opposite and soon turn left on a wide crossing track. **Continue from point 11.**

**10.** Continue straight ahead passing the turning on the left. At the next road junction turn right on the road signposted to Hartfield and Tunbridge Wells. Remain on this road for about ¼ mile and reach a T junction. Cross the road to an enclosed path running to the right of a nursery. You reach the remains of a stile and turn left along the side of a rough field. Pass a gate and reach a stile leading into a wood. Go over a couple of footbridges and later arrive at a road with Colman's Hatch (HN) church on your right. Cross the road to the turning opposite signposted to Wych

Cross, etc. You soon reach a telephone box and bear right on the drive to Shepherds Gate. Ignore a right fork and continue ahead on the tar until this ends, where you go straight ahead over a wide, grassy area, passing a house on your right. Continue on the track, ignoring a right turn and right fork. As you climb steadily the path divides but both tracks lead in the same direction, soon re-joining, and you reach a well-defined crossing track.

**11.** Continue ahead, ascending, with the road over on your left. Go over a wide crossing track by an Ashdown Forest marker post. Pass a wide turning on the right and go over another crossing track. At a fork by a seat turn left and almost immediately right. Continue on this wide track for almost another mile and you will arrive back at the car park with the Ashdown Forest Centre beyond.

### Historical Notes

**Ashdown Forest**, in the Middle Ages, was favoured by kings and the nobility as a hunting ground for the great herds of deer to be found there. Although normally associated with dense woodland, 'forest' originally meant 'hunting area'. However, evidence of man's activity in the area can be traced much further back in time, an axe dating from the Palaeolithic period and flint flakes from Mesolithic workshop sites, together with the occasional finished implement, having been found.

Originally the entire 6,400 acres were wooded but the advent of the Wealden iron industry, with its heavy requirement for timber and charcoal burning, denuded it of half its woodland. It is now primarily of interest for its heathland and during the appropriate season there is an explosion of colour from the mass of gorse, bracken and heather. Thanks to a 1974 Act of Parliament the public have since enjoyed the right to roam over much of it even though it was in private ownership. In 1988 Earl De La Warr sold it to East Sussex County Council, the money being raised by public appeal and national conservation bodies. The Forest is administered by a Board of elected 'Conservators' who have a duty to preserve its unique character for all time.

**Ashdown Park** is a Victorian country house, with later additions, situated in approximately 186 acres of grounds. The original mansion was built in 1815 by Admiral Henniker and at that time the entire estate comprised 3,563 acres. In 1867 Thomas Thompson, Member of Parliament for Durham, bought the estate and demolished most of the existing mansion and was responsible for much of the building you see today. During the First World

War it was used as a hospital for Belgian army officers and after the war, for the next fifty years, as a convent. It has subsequently housed both the United States International University and the Barclays Bank Management Training Centre.

**Chelwood Vachery** was built in 1906 by Sir Stuart Samuel. In 1925 he sold the estate, comprising 101 acres, for £27,000 to a Mr F. J. Nettlefold. It remained in the ownership of the family until purchased by the multinational British-American Tobacco company in 1955 as their Group Management Training Centre. The gardens, which are of great charm and interest, and a blaze of colour in late spring and summer, are open to the public on certain days each year.

**Old Lodge** has recently been completely renovated. In the last century it formed part of the Ashdown Park estate and was for some time the home of Admiral Henniker's widow and later became the property of one of his sons.

**The Enchanted Garden** is dedicated to A(lan) A(lexander) Milne (1882–1956) whose tales of Christopher Robin and his animal friends are told in *Winnie-the-Pooh* (1926) and *The House at Pooh Corner* (1928) and this is where the touching final scenes took place. The views from here are magnificent and over to the right is 500 Acre Wood, known to Christopher Robin as '100 Aker Wood'. Children of all ages brought up with the stories should stop here a minute or two and breathe in the atmosphere. In nearby Hartfield the village shop is called 'Pooh Corner' and it still retains its image as the sweetshop in the stories. A rebuilt 'Pooh Bridge' is also to be found in the area, the original having been worn out by the thousands of 'Pooh' aficionados.

**The Hatch Inn**, positioned as it is in a small cluster of houses, is appreciated by locals and visitors alike. There has been an inn on this site since 1420 but the present building is 17th century and is said to have been the haunt of highwaymen.

**Colman's Hatch**, on the edge of Ashdown Forest, was one of the seven original gateways to the Forest. The name Colman originates from two of the hamlet's inhabitants in the 13th century, Edmund and Richard, who burnt wood for charcoal. 'Hatch' is Old English for gate and in the vicinity you will also find Chuck Hatch and Plaw Hatch, although the one at Chelwood took on the more modern name.

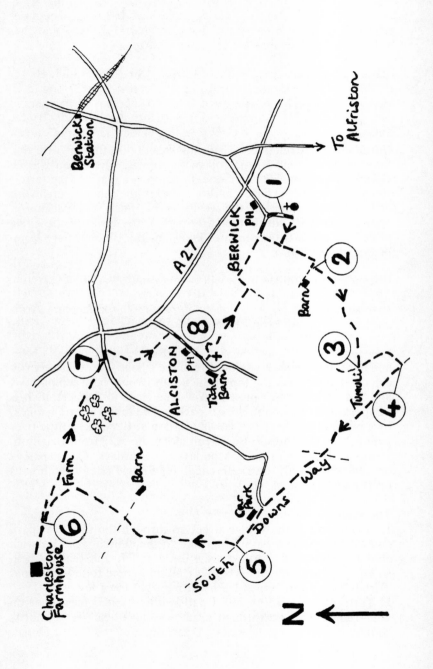

# Berwick and Alciston

**Introduction:** A relatively easy walk, mainly on the flat with one long, gradual climb to the top of the downs where you will be rewarded with fine views. In one direction you may see the ferries steaming out of Newhaven harbour, and in the other a patchwork of farms and villages in the weald below. Such is the seclusion of this area that, during the early part of the century, the circle of literary and artistic intimates known as the Bloomsbury Group made it their own.

**Distance:** This 7 mile circuit will take around 2½–3 hours.

**Refreshments:** There is a pub in Berwick, The Cricketers Arms and another in Alciston, the Rose Cottage.

**How to get there:** Leave the A27 about 8 miles south east of Lewes and park considerately somewhere in the village. Alternatively you can commence from the top of the South Downs between points 4 and 5. Leave the A27 on a narrow lane close to Selmeston. It is signposted 'By Way' and the car park will be found after 1¾ miles, by a picnic site. There is a railway station at Berwick, a little over a mile from the church. Buses run along the A27 from Brighton, Lewes and Eastbourne on Mondays to Saturdays. OS maps 199 or 1308 (TQ 40/50), grid references TQ 519049 (Berwick church) or TQ 494051 (picnic site).

**The Walk**
**1.** At the end of the village street go through the small car park and take the walled path signposted to the church. Pass Berwick church (HN) (well worth a visit) on your left and reach a field where you turn right. Pass a silage pit and come to a T junction. Turn left on a farm track later bearing right for a few yards.
**2.** Turn left onto an enclosed path with a ruined barn over on your right. Later go through a gateway and bear right, shortly coming out to an open area with the slope of the South Downs

ahead. Your track starts to climb fairly steeply and later bears to the right. About halfway up the slope you reach a crossing track with a tumulus ahead.

**3.** Turn left, shortly going through a gate and continue around the hillside, still ascending. You reach the summit and continue straight ahead between barbed-wire fences towards a bridle gate.

**4.** Turn right along the track forming part of the South Downs Way. Go through a bridle gate and follow a wire fence on your left. As the fence curves left you continue ahead over a wide crossing track and pass through a series of gates with a car park on your right and an old barn ahead. Continue along the track for another ¼ mile as far as a bridle gate in the fence on the left.

**5.** Turn sharp right and locate a path bearing left down the hillside to a gate. Continue down the hillside going through a gate at the bottom, then along the left side of a large field with a barn over on your right. Go over a crossing track and continue between fields. Your track becomes concreted as you approach a farm. Once past a barn bear left and reach the drive to Charleston Farmhouse (HN). (If you are visiting Charleston Farmhouse turn left and later retrace your steps.)

**6.** Turn right through a gate and follow the direction of the cables above across a field. Pass some houses on your right and enter another field, shortly going into a third. Travel on into the next field, now with woods on your right and soon pass a business called Keepers on your right. The grass gives way to a concrete track and you come out to a road.

**7.** Turn left for a few yards and then right over a stile signposted Alciston ½ mile. Go down the left side of a field to a stile and over a bridge. Cross the next field diagonally left up a slope to a fence. Continue left to reach the field corner and a pair of stiles. Take the stile on the left and continue ahead on a track which will bring you out to a road. Turn right through the village of Alciston (HN), passing the Rose Cottage pub and in ¼ mile reach a gate leading to the church.

**8.** Go through the gate onto an enclosed path and after going through the next gate turn left through another. Follow the flint wall and go over a stile. Turn right and immediately left heading for the far side of a large field, with a hedge on your left. You will see the spire of Berwick church straight ahead. Turn left along another field and in the corner go over a stile. Turn right following a fence on your right and reach a concreted farm track. Continue ahead passing a large barn on your right and go down to a lane and a grass triangle. Turn right along the lane back towards the church.

## Historical Notes

**Berwick church** is an absolute must for a visit. Here you will find a wall painting with a difference. During World War II the Bishop of Chichester commissioned local artists, members of the Bloomsbury Group, to paint a contemporary mural on the walls of the 12th century church. The brilliant painting includes the portraits of many local characters including a soldier, sailor and airman. At the time the portrayal of angels with fashionable 1940s hair-dos caused considerable controversy.

**Charleston Farmhouse** was the weekend retreat for many members of the Bloomsbury Group and later the retirement home for a few of them. The house is now open on certain days and contains much memorabilia of the period. (There are also some toilets which may be useful at this point on the walk!)

**Alciston**, pronounced A'ston by true locals, consists of a single street of old thatch and timber houses ending at the foot of the downs with a church and farm which includes the remains of a 14th century abbey. The 170 ft tithe barn is claimed to be the largest in the county. Rose Cottage public house was a private residence until the end of the last century, which explains its unusual name. If you should happen to be here on a Good Friday you may be expected to stop walking and start skipping. As many as 20 people at a time line up to jump over a long rope. This event has religious origins, the rope representing the one that Judas Iscariot used to hang himself after his betrayal of Christ.

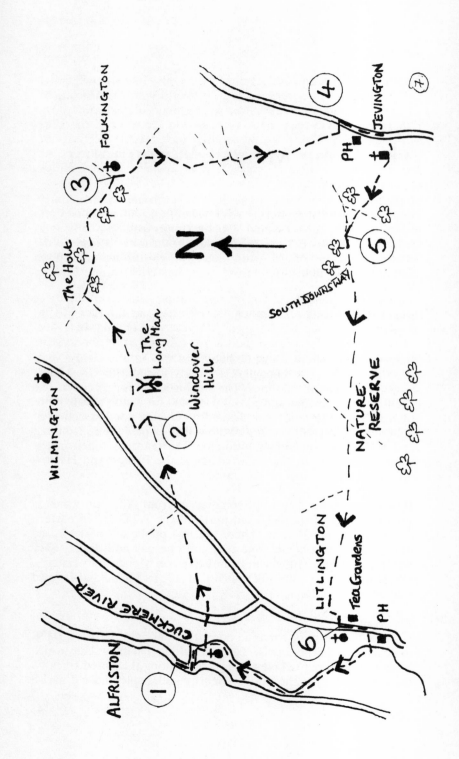

# Alfriston and The Long Man of Wilmington

**Introduction:** A moderately energetic walk through varied country-side. There is a meandering river valley, ancient woodland and inviting heath and downland. Gentle climbs lead you to superb, panoramic views. Besides having the opportunity to explore the charming village of Alfriston you will go through Jevington and Litlington and pass close to the mysterious Long Man of Wilmington.

**Distance:** The walk is about 9 miles, circular, and will take around 3½–4 hours.

**Refreshments:** There are three pubs in Alfriston, the George Inn, the Star Inn and The Smugglers (formerly The Market Cross Inn), as well as shops and tea shops (The Singing Kettle is very cosy). The Eight Bells in Jevington is usefully located for a stop a little more than halfway through the walk and it serves a good selection of light meals. Towards the end of the walk you pass the welcoming, and highly recommended, Litlington Tea Gardens, open in the summer months. In the same village is the Plough and Harrow pub, only a few yards off the route.

**How to get there:** The walk commences from Alfriston which is situated south of the A27 and north of the A259 at the eastern end of the South Downs. There are two public car parks at the north end of the village, one free and one pay and display. Try the free one first! Buses run from Lewes on Mondays to Fridays. OS Maps 199 or 1308 (TQ 40/50) or 1324 (TV 49/59/69), grid reference TQ 521033.

### The Walk
**1.** From the car park continue down the road into Alfriston (HN) to reach the market cross. Turn left along a narrow lane which leads to the river Cuckmere. Turn right along the raised track by the river and cross the bridge. Nearby is the splendid old parish

church fronting the village green which is known as The Tye. Once over the river continue ahead to a road which you cross, slightly right, to a gate and a path signposted to Jevington and Lullington. Go up some steps and in about 100 yards bear left to a stile and then go diagonally right across a field. Go over another stile and maintain direction across the next field. The next stile leads to a track, forming part of the South Downs Way (HN – Walk 2), where you turn right and soon cross a road. Go through a bridle gate and continue uphill towards a reservoir. A 100 yards further on you come to a bridle gate.

**2.** Turn sharp left, leaving the South Downs Way (SDW), and go along the side of a fence for about 50 yards. Bear right at an obvious turn and go along the hillside heading towards another bridle gate. Continue along the well-defined track and later Wilmington church (HN) will come into view on your far left as will The Long Man of Wilmington (HN), carved in the chalk, on your close right. Keeping the fence on your right, use any of the continuing parallel tracks along the hillside to the point where they all merge together and then proceed on the single track to a bridle gate. Continue into the woodland of The Holt where you join a track coming in from the left and in about ½ mile you will reach a junction of paths at Folkington church (HN).

**3.** Turn right on a bridleway and remain on this for about 250 yards to a waymark on a post. The direction of the waymark and line on the map suggests that you should bear diagonally right across the large field in a southerly direction. However, if the field is ploughed or cropped you may find it easier to turn right on a track between fields for about 150 yards and, where you meet a fence, bear left across the field. Either way, aim for a stile in the fence in front of a steep bank. Bear right up the bank to another stile at the top and maintain direction towards a post marker in the middle of the next field. The next stile leads you to some steps and through an area of shrubbery. You will notice a house over on your left as you join a bridleway and turn right for a few yards and then left again back onto a footpath. The next stile leads you onto an enclosed footpath between paddocks and another stile back onto a bridleway again. Bear right and in a few yards turn left soon going up some steps and over a stile. Continue across a field to stiles each side of a crossing farm track. Head in the direction of a white house and your path becomes enclosed. After going over a stile, turn right on a diverted path to reach a farm track. Turn left for a short distance to reach a road in the village of Jevington.

**4.** Turn right along the road, soon passing (or maybe entering)

The Eight Bells (plastic bags are provided for muddy boots!). The footpath reaches some railings and you are gently led, right, into the churchyard of Jevington church (HN). Keep the church on your right and join a bridleway bearing right, back onto the SDW. You start to climb along the edge of some woodland and reach a crossing track by a SDW sign. Continue ahead and shortly reach a T junction.

**5.** Turn left, still on the SDW, but at the next signpost, where the Way bears off to the right, you keep straight ahead. You are led onto Lullington Heath National Nature Reserve where there is an information board and map by a left fork. You keep to the main, undulating path, where later a track comes in from the right and you pass another information board on the left. (Winchester Pond – a dew pond – is hidden away on your right.) Continue ahead for another mile, ignoring a bridleway forking right to Lullington Court, and eventually bear left and then right through a farmyard to the road in the village of Litlington (HN).

**6.** Turn left along the road, soon passing the church on your right and Litlington Tea Gardens on the left. Opposite Holly Tree House (the Plough and Harrow pub is a few more yards down the road) turn right on a tarred public footpath which bears left to a footbridge over the river Cuckmere. Once over the bridge turn immediately right towards a stile and continue along the river bank. You go over a series of stiles and later pass Alfriston church. You are soon back in the attractive village, possibly with time to explore some of its delights.

### Historical Notes

**Alfriston** is a very quaint village and well worth investigating. The spacious church is late 14th century and has been described as 'the cathedral of the South Downs'. The Clergy House, also 14th century, is timber-framed and thatched and was the first building bought by the National Trust in 1896 – for just £10!

In the past the village was notorious for its smuggling activity and was the home of the Alfriston Gang, led by one Stanton Collins who lived at The Market Cross Inn. Six staircases and 48 doors led into 21 rooms making the building an ideal hiding place for both the illicit goods and those who chose to trade in the lucrative business. Cuckmere Haven on the coast a couple of miles down river from the village was the perfect unofficial port serving this early form of black marketing.

**Wilmington church** is 11th century and has a curious 'insect window' depicting St. Peter in the midst of bees, butterflies and moths. In the churchyard is a giant, twin-trunked yew, claimed to be 1,000 years old.

**The Long Man of Wilmington** overlooks the village on the side of Windover Hill. He stands 227 ft high grasping two staves a little longer than himself. No one seems to know when the figure was carved, or why. Does he originate from the Neolithic period, did the Romans play a part in his carving, or was it the work of monks from the nearby priory? There are several theories about his identity. Is he a giant slain on the spot by a hammer thrown by another giant who lived at Firle or could he be Woden, the Norse god of war?

**Folkington church** still has some oak box pews, one on two levels and two with a central rail for hymn books. On the north wall there is a monument to Viscount Monckton. As Sir Walter Monckton he was adviser to King Edward VIII during the Abdication crisis and he lived opposite the church in the Old Rectory. His wife was a great lover of badgers and introduced the legislation which later became the Badger Protection Act.

**Jevington church** has a strange Saxon carving inside thought to be of Christ fighting the devil in the form of a wild beast. In the graveyard you may like to seek out a bronze memorial to a Liverpool shipowner in the form of a fully-rigged frigate, complete with lifeboats and cannons. A century or two ago many of the tombs were utilised by smugglers as storage places for their contraband.

**Litlington** proudly claims to have introduced the county's first tea garden which still thrives today.

If you visit the church you will discover a low and minuscule door in the north wall leading to a confined, winding staircase to the belfry illuminated only by tiny slits in the wall. Outside, search for no less than three sundials, two on the north west buttress and the other on the south porch.

# Exceat
# and Friston Forest

**Introduction:** Any climbs on this walk are gradual ones or have steps to assist you, making this a fairly easy walk. Given a clear day the panoramas over the Cuckmere valley will be quite spectacular as you follow the ridge path to the viewpoint at High and Over. You will go through the village of Litlington with its interesting church and then gently climb up to Lullington Heath Nature Reserve, enjoying more good views along the way. An extremely pleasant spot to stop for a picnic is at the easily missed Winchester Pond from where you descend into Friston Forest on your way to the village of West Dean with its ancient rectory.

**Distance:** This approximately 8 mile circuit will take about 3 hours. This does not include stopping time, so allow extra if you like to tarry and soak in the scenery.

**Refreshments:** At Exceat you have the Seven Sisters Country Park tea shop as well as The Golden Galleon pub/restaurant. In Litlington the Plough and Harrow pub serves food lunchtimes and evenings and the well-known tea gardens are open from the beginning of April until the end of October.

**How to get there:** The car park at Exceat is on the seaward side of the A259 Seaford–Eastbourne road, opposite the Seven Sisters Country Park Information Centre, where there are toilets. Buses run from Brighton and Eastbourne via Seaford on Mondays to Saturdays. OS maps 199 or 1324 (TV 49/59/69), grid reference TV 519994.

### The Walk
**1.** From the car park turn left along the main road for about ¼ mile and cross the river Cuckmere via the road bridge. Bear right with the road and in about 150 yards cross over a stile on the right. Proceed on a footpath and soon bear left to continue along the river bank for about ½ mile where you will come to a stile.

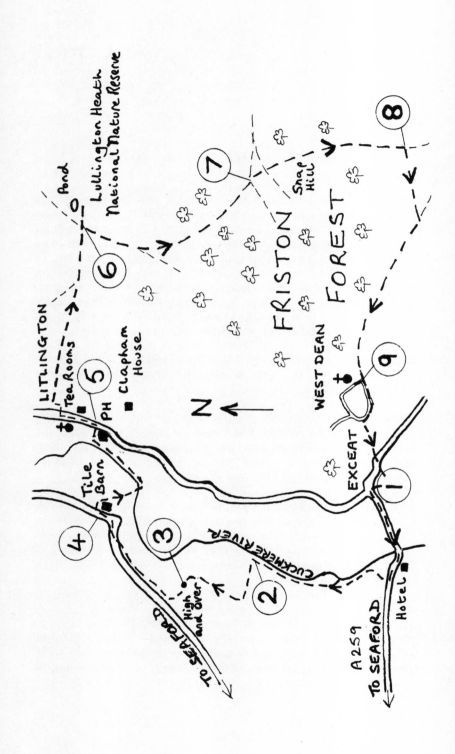

**2.** After crossing the stile continue ahead for a few yards past bushes and then turn sharp left up the side of a field. Before reaching a stile by a gate at the top of the field look left to admire the view of the Cuckmere estuary. You do not cross the stile but turn right along a fine ridge path with a fence on your left. Cross a stile and soon reach another where you turn left and go up some steps to arrive at the viewpoint of High and Over.

**3.** From the viewpoint continue ahead on a path going through bushes and trees and, on reaching a junction of paths, bear right past a seat and reach a T junction. Turn right downhill and go over a stile continuing past the tumuli which form an ancient burial ground. Go on downhill to a stile and proceed on an enclosed path and out to a road. Cross the road and make your way downhill on a grassy path. The road turns sharply left and, at the bottom of the slope, you will reach the well-preserved ancient Tile Barn at Frog Firle.

**4.** Cross the road to pass the barn and its adjacent buildings on your right. Go through a gate and immediately turn right through two more. Bear half right up a slope and join a track, keeping right at a fork, still uphill. Go steeply downhill to a bridge and cross over the river. Use the stile on the left and continue along the river bank, then over another stile and past a footbridge to join a tarred path. The path soon bears right and brings you onto a road in the village of Litlington (HN – Walk 7). (The Plough and Harrow pub is a few yards to your right.)

**5.** Turn left, soon passing (or using!) the tea gardens on your right and go on past the church (HN – Walk 7). Very shortly cross the road and turn right through a farmyard on a bridleway signposted to Jevington. Soon bear left past a cowshed and then right to continue on a well-defined track where you commence to climb steadily. Shortly over on your right you may see Clapham House (HN) through the trees. After about ½ mile a track comes in from the left by a signpost and you keep ahead. When your path forks keep right past a Lullington Heath National Nature Reserve information board and continue for a few yards. Bear left and you will find a dew pond called Winchester Pond. Retrace your steps back to the path junction.

**6.** Turn left (south) on the track signposted to Charleston Bottom. When you reach an enclosed weather station on your left turn left to another fine viewpoint (and good place for your picnic!). Return to your original track and later commence descending. At a fork keep left, continuing in a south-easterly direction, still going downhill. The slope becomes more steep and you reach a junction of paths.

**7.** Take the path signposted to Snap Hill. (Do not be confused by the waymark here which may suggest to you that your route is the wide, grassy track straight ahead.) Bear right uphill in a south-easterly direction and, at the next junction, fork slightly right on the path signposted to Friston and West Dean going fairly steeply uphill. Towards the top of the slope go over a wide crossing track and continue ahead, your direction now being slightly east of south. Pass a turning on your left and start descending soon passing a turning on the right with a tall building on the horizon ahead. Still descending you go down to a forestry road which you cross, continuing up the slope waymarked to Friston. Your path is wide and grassy as you go through an area of deforestation. Way over on your right you may catch a glimpse of Seaford bay. Eventually you reach a large open area of grassland.

**8.** Ignore the Friston waymark and turn right along a wide track with trees on your right. At the end of this open area bear right on a descending, grassy path. Later you re-cross the forestry road, now following the West Dean waymark and going uphill. Another forestry road comes in from your right and you continue ahead on it. When you reach the point where the road bears right downhill, continue straight ahead on a wide track towards a house. Your track becomes tarred as you continue downhill to a sharp bend on a lane in the village of West Dean (HN).

**9.** Turn right along the lane to see the rectory and then retrace your steps to the bend. Turn right and soon pass an ancient dovecote on your right. Pass The Old Schoolhouse and bear right. As the lane bears right again turn left past a telephone box and go up a long flight of steps with a South Downs Way acorn waymark. You reach a stone wall and a stile which you cross. Go through a gate and downhill across a field, then over a stile by a gate and out to the road which you cross to the car park opposite.

**Historical Notes**

**Exceat**, spelt 'Excete' on old maps and correctly pronounced 'Exseat', not 'Exy-at', was once an important fishing village and also an important point of entry for smuggled brandy on its way to the illicit distribution centre up the river Cuckmere at Alfriston. Frequent raiders from France decimated the population in the early 16th century and in 1528 the parish became incorporated into adjacent West Dean. Tourist attractions in the area are the Seven Sisters Country Park Information Centre which is well worth a visit as is the nearby museum, The Living World, displaying live insects, fish and a variety of other small creatures.

**Clapham House** was the home of Mrs Maria Fitzherbert before she married and was later deserted by King George IV (who was Prince Regent at the time). It is claimed that, such was his ardour, he rode the 18 miles from Brighton to visit her.

**Friston Forest** was once densely wooded but was cleared for grazing centuries ago. The present forest is a mixture of cultivated beech and non-indigenous conifer. The huge plantation was started in the last century in order to protect the quality of the water supply to Eastbourne and the surrounding area.

**West Dean** is a delightful conservation village, well-hidden in a corner of Friston Forest. The rectory is claimed to be the oldest inhabited one in the country. With walls $2\frac{1}{2}$ ft thick and a stone spiral staircase, part of it dates from 1220. The magnificent circular flint dovecote would once have had a conical roof and the wall around also once protected the manor house, parts of which are still visible. It is claimed that Alfred the Great had a palace here. Certainly his biographer Asser the monk, who later became a bishop, was summoned here and documented his royal welcome.

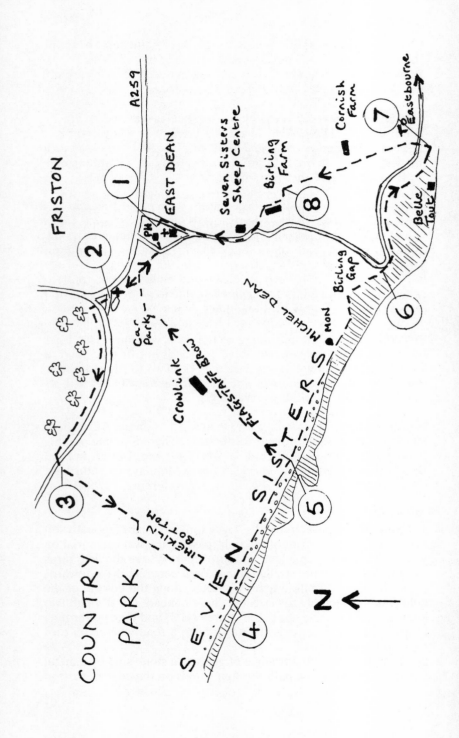

# East Dean and
# The Seven Sisters

**Introduction:** There are very attractive sea views for most of this moderately energetic walk. The route skirts Friston Forest and follows the fine coastal path going over six of the famous Seven Sisters cliffs. On a clear day you will be able to see far along the south coast and even glimpse the Isle of Wight some 50 miles away.

**Distance:** The full route is 7 miles but this may be reduced to 4 miles, taking 3 or 2 hours respectively.

**Refreshments:** At the beginning of the walk you have The Tiger Inn which will be pleased to serve you with hot or cold food at lunchtime or evenings, seven days a week. Two thirds of the way round the full route you will find the Birling Gap Hotel with its café serving snacks all day, every day.

**How to get there:** Start from East Dean which is on the A259 about halfway between Seaford and Eastbourne. There is ample parking in the public car park at the side of The Tiger Inn. Buses run from Brighton and Eastbourne via Seaford on Mondays to Saturdays. OS maps 199 or 1324 (TV 49/59/69), grid reference TV 557978.

**The Walk**
**1.** From the car park go to The Tiger Inn and bear diagonally left across the green in front of the pub, passing the war memorial on your right. You reach a lane and turn right. Where the lane turns sharply right continue straight ahead on a concrete drive towards a gate leading you into a field. Continue along the bottom of the field climbing steadily towards the church ahead. Go through two kissing gates to arrive at Friston church (HN) and then go through a rare, pivoting gate (tapsell gate), out to a road where you turn right to the main road.
**2.** Cross the road and a triangle of grass to a stone stile by a metal barrier. Continue on a path through woods on the edge of Friston

Forest (HN – Walk 8). The path soon descends and you keep left at a fork. Continue for about ¾ mile on this path which runs more or less parallel to the road over on your left and with a steep slope on your right. You reach an open grassy area with a log seat where you leave the path to cross the road. Turn right for a few yards.

**3.** Go through a kissing gate at the entrance to New Barn Cottage. You are now in the Seven Sisters Country Park. Bear right across the field ahead in a south-westerly direction, passing barns over on your right, and reach a stile in the corner. Cross the stile and continue along the left side of the next field with a fence on your left and later the path bears to the right, still with the fence on your left. You are led to another stile which you cross maintaining your original direction towards the coast ahead. Go over another stile and straight ahead to the next stile which leads you to an open area of the Seven Sisters and the South Downs Way (footpath route).

**4.** Turn left down the slope of Limekiln Bottom and then climb up the slope of Rough Brow. Go down to Rough Bottom and keep ahead as the next climb takes you up to Brass Point. A stile takes you into the National Trust area of Crowlink (HN). You go down again to Gap Bottom where there is a left turn. Ahead is your next climb up to a sarsen stone donated by the Society of Sussex Downsmen.

**5. For the 4 mile walk continue as follows:** Turn left along the ridge of Flagstaff Brow and in about a mile, after passing the settlement of Crowlink down on your left, you will go through a kissing gate by a cattle grid into a car park. At the top of this turn right through a kissing gate and then bear left to the bottom of a field. Retrace the steps of your outward route, later going through a gate and maintaining direction along the lane back to The Tiger Inn.

**For the full 7 mile walk:** Continue ahead on the coastal path for another ¾ mile going up and over another three of the Seven Sisters. At Michel Dean you pass a monument in memory of three young officers killed in World War I; the surrounding land was bequeathed to The National Trust by their family. You go through a gate and bear left, away from the coast, to a wooden barrier. Turn right to a metal barrier and continue down an unmade road to Birling Gap (HN) with its café and toilets.

**6.** From Birling Gap join a path which, at first, runs parallel with a road on your left. Belle Tout (HN), a former lighthouse, comes into view and your path bears away from the road and you continue for about ½ mile where you go through two old gateposts.

**7.** Turn sharp left down a bank and across the road to join the concreted drive of Cornish Farm. As you come close to farm buildings and the drive bears right you continue straight ahead through two bridle gates and onto a farm track running between fields. Later you go through a farm gate and follow a stone wall on your left to reach another bridle gate.

**8.** Turn left towards Birling Farm passing a large barn on your left and keeping to the right of a fence. Go through another gate by a house. The next gate leads you out to the farm drive on which you bear right out towards a road. Proceed past the Seven Sisters Sheep Centre (which also serves teas) and continue along the road. Pass a turning on the left and just beyond East Dean church (HN) you will find the car park on your left.

## Historical Notes

**East Dean** was once an important link between Britain and the continent, the first cable office being located here. The building still stands and wires from it were carried on telegraph poles to connect with undersea cables leaving from Birling Gap.

The Tiger Inn, part of a row of flint buildings, once formed the barracks housing local militia. The inn took its name from the leopard on the Bardolf coat of arms, the distinction between these big cats obviously being lost to most in the 16th century.

The church registers contain the amazing story of Agnes and Joan Payne, buried here in 1796. Agnes, the elder, was taken ill and lay speechless for 24 hours, evidently near to death. Then suddenly she called out for her sister to come with her. Joan was in good health but within half an hour she also became ill. The following morning they died together and this story was confirmed by the vicar and churchwardens.

**Friston church** shows evidence of early vandalism. In the stone porch you will find graffiti crudely carved centuries ago. The porch door is dedicated to the memory of Frank Bridge, the conductor who occasionally deputised for Sir Henry Wood at the Proms. The Reverend A. A. Evans, vicar from 1908 to 1929, was a keen country walker and wrote many delightful books on the subject, including *One Foot in Sussex* and *By Weald and Down*.

**Crowlink**, 'The Hill of Crows' is an estate village which was in the ownership of the Payn family for many generations. Now in the care of The National Trust, it was once the home of E. Nesbit, author of *The Railway Children*. A century or two ago the cellars of Crowlink House reputedly stored 'Genuine Crowlink' – an expensive smuggled gin.

**Birling Gap**, where the first telephone cables connected England to France, was once a haven for smugglers operating from East Dean.

**Belle Tout**, dating from 1831, enjoys a prominent position up on the cliffs. Now used as a private residence, it was once a lighthouse. Unfortunately, being fogbound for much of the winter, the light had to be moved to its newer home at Beachy Head. In the early 18th century the local vicar hollowed out a cavern in the cliff side with steps down to the beach which could be used as a refuge for shipwrecked sailors.

# Groombridge
# and Harrison's Rocks

**Introduction:** The walk commences from Groombridge, a pleasant village of 18th century tiled cottages close to the Kent border and only a few miles from Tunbridge Wells. The few climbs are all very gentle and lead to fine Wealden views over both counties. You will pass close to Harrison's Rocks which provide good training for aspiring mountaineers.

**Distance:** This circular route of around 7 miles will take 3–3½ hours.

**Refreshments:** There is a village store and a bakery in Groombridge as well as The Junction pub. To the north of the village you will find The Crown which serves real ales. A short diversion, but after only a quarter of the walk, will bring you to The Huntsman pub near Eridge station.

**How to get there:** The walk commences from the (free) village car park, opposite the post office. Groombridge is on the B2110 which runs south from the A264 East Grinstead–Tunbridge Wells road. Nearby is Eridge station on the Uckfield line and buses run via Crowborough from Nutley and Uckfield. OS maps 188 or 1248 (TQ 43/53), grid reference TQ 531373.

**The Walk**
**1.** From the car park turn left down the village street passing the former railway station (HN) as you cross over the bridge. Follow the road out of the village and, in ¼ mile, fork right along the road signposted to Eridge station. In about 200 yards, immediately before some houses, turn right along a track that leads into the Forestry Commission's Birchden Wood. It will bring you to a parking area (where there are toilets) for visitors to Harrison's Rocks (HN).
**2.** At the bottom left corner of the car park take a path to a waymarked stile leading into a field. Bear left and soon left

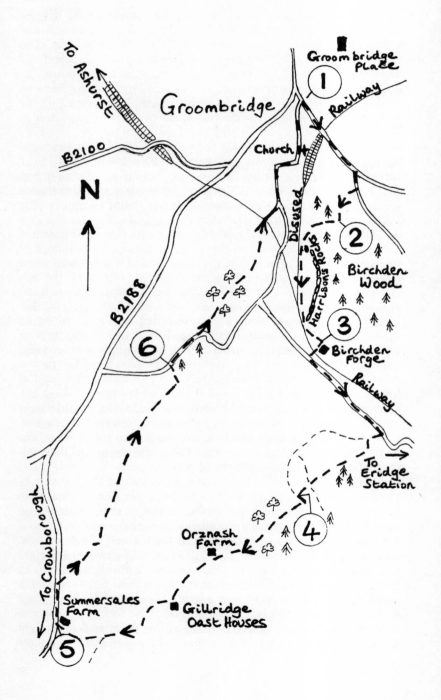

again into another field and follow a path parallel to the disused railway line over on your right. Later you are close to the railway embankment with Harrison's Rocks well in view on the left. You pass by a railway junction and go through a gate into woodland and shortly arrive at Birchden Forge, a converted oast house.

**3.** Turn right alongside the house and cross the railway line and a stream, coming out to a quiet country lane. Turn left along the lane for about ½ mile where you reach the drive signposted to Motts Farm. Eridge station and The Huntsman pub are less than ½ mile ahead but to continue the walk you turn right here and shortly pass a large house on your left. Just beyond the house turn left through a farmyard and then bear right across a hop field. Pass a wood on your left and go straight over two more fields. You continue over a crossing track, with fingerposts, and across another field to a T junction.

**4.** Turn left on a farm track which soon bears right and continue for another ½ mile or so to reach the entrance and buildings of Orznash Farm. Continue on the farm track which bears right and left and, after passing by some orchards, you reach the two charming Gillridge oast houses. The drive beyond is surfaced and later, by the track leading to Stonecroft Farm, it bears left. Leave the drive by crossing a stile and then follow the direction of the fingerpost downhill across a paddock and to the right of an all-weather training enclosure. You soon reach a stile, cross a planked bridge and bear right on the path running past a pond. Cross two metal pole barriers and reach the main road at Summersales Farm.

**5.** Turn right along the road for about ¼ mile where you turn right through a gate onto an enclosed path and reach a stile on the left. Cross this stile and then another. Cut across the corner of a field to the edge of a wood. Turn right for a few yards and then left to continue along the left side of a large field. You pass a left turning leading to Park Grove and continue along the left side of the next field. Go through a substantial squeeze stile and maintain direction, following a line of trees, passing a rocky outcrop on your left and then entering woodland. Descend diagonally across a meadow, go over a stile and then through a belt of trees. Cross a drive and keep ahead for 20 yards. A stream flows to the right and you descend to cross it. Once over a footbridge turn left to find and cross another in the corner of the field. Climb to a stile at the top of a slope and reach a lane.

**6.** Turn right along the lane and continue to the foot of a hill where it turns sharply right. Leave the lane at this point and go straight ahead, passing to the left of a garage, and enter woodland. Follow a path through woods and along a sloping strip of grassland. At the far end go over two stiles and cross a cultivated field to pass through a railway arch. Continue across grass to reach a road by a waterworks. Turn left and follow the road, which turns right and left, passing Groombridge church (HN), back into the village.

**Historical Notes**

**Groombridge** grew up around the railway station. On the north side of the village lies Groombridge Place, the local manor house. Five hundred years ago this was in the ownership of Richard Waller who fought the French and brought back the uncle of Louis XII as a hostage. The unfortunate Frenchman was held here until the ransom was paid – some 33 years later!

**The railway line**, until a few years ago, linked the London–Hastings line with the London–Uckfield line at Tunbridge Wells. The station building is still intact, but now houses commercial offices. It is intended to re-open the line as a private railway and volunteers work on it every weekend. The headquarters of TWERPS (the Tunbridge Wells and Eridge Railway Preservation Society) is based at Eridge station. Visitors can see how work is progressing on the project as well as peruse a fine collection of railway books and other associated memorabilia.

**Harrison's Rocks** are formed of sandstone, with deep cracks, chimneys and bulging overhangs, reaching heights of up to 45 ft. They are very popular with climbers owing to their relatively close proximity to London.

**Groombridge church**, dedicated to St. Thomas the Apostle, was built between 1883 and 1884 and designed by Richard Norman Shaw. This influential architect revolted against the prevailing High Victorian style of the 1870s. Instead, he used the perpendicular style and materials which included locally quarried sandstone similar to that found at Harrison's Rocks.

# Mark Cross
# and Best Beech Hill

**Introduction:** When you have attempted all the other walks in this book and you feel ready to try something a little longer and more energetic, this is the walk for you. Much of the route is on the Sussex Border Path, closely following the Kent boundary. Sections of the Path are included in several of our walks but this one takes in a considerable stretch, about 5 miles in all. The walk traverses a network of streams so that you are never far from the gurgle of water. Here is a pleasant day out for any time of the year but especially autumn when the tree colours are glorious.

**Distance:** Allow a full day to complete this 12 mile circuit for which the walking time will be around $5\frac{1}{2}$–6 hours.

**Refreshments:** In Mark Cross you have the Mark Cross Inn and, conveniently situated about two-thirds of the way round, you will find the Best Beech Inn which has a good selection of snacks and more substantial meals and a warming, open fire on cold, winter days.

**How to get there:** Leave the A267 Mayfield–Tunbridge Wells road at Mark Cross and you will find a small car park at the side of the Magistrate's Court and almost opposite the pub. Buses run from Heathfield and Tunbridge Wells. Wadhurst station on the Tunbridge Wells–Hastings line could be used to join the walk at point 9. OS maps 188 or 1248 (TQ 43/53), 1249 (TQ 63/73), 1270 (TQ 62/72) and 1269 (TQ 42/52) tiny part only, grid reference TQ 582311.

**The Walk**
**1.** From the car park bear left along the road through the village and reach the main road which you cross to a public footpath sign opposite. Go down a bank and along an enclosed path with a garden centre on the right. Continue along the left side of a field, later going over a stile and bearing right across the next field. Keep

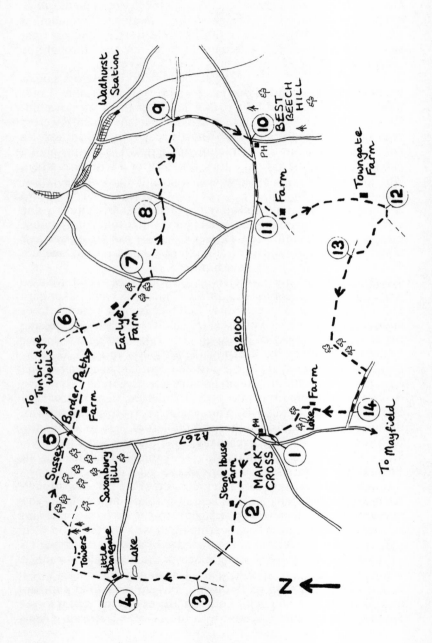

left at a fork and go over another stile and then alongside a ditch. Cross a stream and, later, a stile, continuing between fields. Once over the next stile you go straight across a large field into another where you bear half right and cross the next stile. Go along the right side of a field, passing a gate on your right, and then through the gate ahead. Stone House Farm is over to your right.

**2.** Turn immediately right over a stile and bear right across a field, heading for the second of two gates where you cross a stile. Enter a bracken-covered area on a path which later turns left downhill. Eventually turn left over a bridge and out to a lane which you cross onto the driveway to Entry Hill. Shortly reach a house and stables and, at a fork, keep left continuing on a path leading through a gate and straight ahead. At a fork bear left for a few yards where you will reach a crossing track and a tree marked with a yellow blob.

**3.** Turn right and soon cross a bridge, then join a wide track going uphill. You ascend on this rocky path for about ½ mile, past a house on the left, and continue on a tarred driveway passing a pond and a lake to reach a road. Bear left up the road past Little Danegate and shortly reach a footpath signpost.

**4.** Turn right into a field with a fence on your right. You have now joined a section of the Sussex Border Path (HN) and Saxonbury Hill (HN) is over on your right. Later bear right beneath trees and reach a fork where you keep left and then bear right, passing two towers on your right. Bear right, soon descending to a sleeper bridge taking you over a stream, and then climb up again. Go over a wide crossing track at a fingerpost and continue ahead along the edge of a wood with the stream on your left. Eventually you leave the wood and come out into a field and bear right following a line of blue and white posts. You reach a footpath signpost by an opening in a fence and you keep to the left of this, following the fence on your right, and eventually come out to a road.

**5.** Cross the road, slightly right, and join a track leading to Pococksgate Farm. Pass the farmhouse on your right and go through a gate heading along the left side of a field. Go through the next gate and along the next field. The following gate takes you into an orchard which you go straight across. Leave via a gate and continue along the next field bearing right, with the fence on your left, and cross a stile. Go along the edge of a field and through a metal farm gate. Proceed straight across the next field towards a white house and reach a stile which you should not cross.

**6.** Turn right and soon go through a squeeze stile, then another, and down the side of a field. Follow a line of electric cables to yet another squeeze stile followed by a bridge over a stream. Climb up from the bank on a steep slope with the aid of rocks which form rough steps. Enter a field and bear left towards farm buildings. Pass between barns and go through a metal gate. Bear left and then right towards an oast house and after passing this bear right to a gate with a waymark. Continue along the left side of a field and at the bottom look out for a memorial stone on your right as you enter woods via a squeeze stile. Descend on a steep, rocky path and shortly you reach a lane.

7. Turn right down the lane for about 100 yards and find a stile on your left which you cross. Soon go over a bridge and climb a rocky path. Go over a crossing track and continue up to cross a stile, then maintain direction up a field with a fence on your right. Go over another stile and proceed with the fence now on your left. Cross the next stile to the left of a wooden farm gate and maintain direction. Cross the next field and at the end of this go over a stile and bear left across another field, soon ignoring a left fork. The next stile takes you out to a road.

8. Turn left and in about 50 yards, opposite Buckhurst Lodge, turn right over a stile and bear left across a field and over the next stile. Bear left and then right, following the direction of a waymark down towards a stream which you cross via a plank bridge. Bear slightly left across the next field and go through a gateway. Cross another field and the next stile. Continue with a stream down on your left and later your path crosses over it. (Be careful here as the rocks may be slippery!) You come out to a field and soon cross a stile turning left on a farm track. In about 1/4 mile, reach a road. The Sussex Border Path continues along the road opposite but you leave it here.

9. Turn right down the road, passing a path turning right, and in a little over 1/4 mile, where the road curves right, continue straight ahead on a tarred track which brings you out to a road with the Best Beech Inn opposite.

10. Turn right along the road, passing a turning on the right and later passing the entrance to Pennybridge Farm on the left. Also on the left shortly find the track to Bensfield Farm.

11. Turn left and continue past Bensfield Farm Cottages on a concreted driveway. Ignore a right fork and continue on the concrete for just a few yards and then go straight ahead on a farm track towards a waymarked post. Go through a gateway and continue across a field, through a metal gate and straight across the next field, passing one gate to arrive at another with a waymark. Follow on across a field and then into another with a steep slope down on your left. If you look well over to your left, on a clear day you should spot the spire of Wadhurst church. Go

through another gate and continue on a farm track towards some houses. After passing them bear right over a stile. Go down the left side of a field, then over a stile and down the next field. The following stile takes you onto an enclosed path and you then go over a plank bridge and reach a tarred farm track.

**12.** Turn right past a white house and bear right on a bridleway. Go through a gate and turn left over a stream into a field and turn right. Pass a pond on your right, go through a gate and continue along the next field to another gate leading into the next field, still following the stream on your right. Bear right to the next gate and reach a wide crossing track.

**13.** Turn left and later go through a farm gate by a stream. Continue along the side of a field, ascending slightly. Later the main track bears left but you go through the gate ahead and immediately turn left over a stile. Bear right and go through a gate by a fingerpost. Continue along the left side of three more fields and turn left through a gate beneath trees. Ascend on a wide track and shortly you will find a horse ride running parallel on your left. Go through a gate and over a stile onto an enclosed path, through a farmyard, and out to a road. Turn right along the road for about ¼ mile to reach a footpath sign by a metal gate on your right.

**14.** Turn right and follow along the left side of a field, bearing left across the next field towards a gate to the right of a farmyard. Continue straight on through the farmyard, passing large barns and the farmhouse on your right and shortly reach a farm gate. Provision for a stile was being made here. If this now exists turn left over the stile and continue under trees, passing an attractive lake on your left and then turn right over a fence. Otherwise go through the gate and turn left along the side of a field to its corner. Continue with the fence on your left and cross a stile. Go over a ditch and up the right side of a field to reach a gate; the car park at Mark Cross is opposite.

**Historical Notes**

**The Sussex Border Path** is a long distance footpath, covering almost 150 miles of the inland boundaries of both counties with Hampshire, Surrey and Kent as well as with each other. It was originally conceived in 1980 as a contrast to the chalk ridges of the North and South Downs which also lent themselves to two long distance paths in this south-east corner of England. The Wealden area between these two ridges offers splendid and contrasting scenery and, although the path follows the borders as closely as possible, the most scenic paths available have been used and road-walking is avoided as much as possible.

**Saxonbury Hill**, at 625 ft, is an excellent example of the few pre-Roman camps to be found in the forested parts of Sussex. Archaeologists have discovered much evidence of a very busy Iron Age hillfort on the top. An easily-traceable ditch surrounded the site which for over 100 years was used for iron-mining and smelting. On the summit is a tower, complete with arrow slits, similar to the two passed on the walk and suggesting medieval origins. In truth it is a folly built in 1828 by a local landowner, Henry Abergavenny.

# Warbleton
# and Rushlake Green

**Introduction:** Walkers find this particularly unspoilt part of the county ideal for exercise and solitude. It is a haven for an abundance of wildlife in summer and the observant visitor will find much of interest during the other seasons, too. Although mainly on gentle paths, some amount of agility will be required to climb barriers where stiles have yet to be installed.

**Distance:** The full circuit of 6 miles will take around 2½–3 hours but this may be reduced to 3 or 4 miles, taking 1½ or 2 hours respectively.

**Refreshments:** About two-thirds of the way round the full walk or halfway round the 4 mile one, you have, in Rushlake Green, the 16th century Horse and Groom and the village stores selling confectionery and ice cream. At the end you have The War Bill-In-Tun (HN). Both pubs are very cosy and serve hot and cold meals and bar snacks at lunchtime every day and each evening apart from Sunday.

**How to get there:** The walk commences from Warbleton church which is signposted off the B2096 which in turn leaves the A265 just east of Heathfield. There is parking by the church entrance and opposite the nearby pub. Buses run to Rushlake Green (point 8) from Battle on weekdays only. OS maps 199 or 1290 (TQ 61/71), grid reference TQ 609182.

### The Walk
**1.** Go up the road and immediately after passing the church (HN) turn left into a field towards a fingerpost with waymarks. If possible, follow the direction of the waymark pointing right and cross the field. You descend to continue with a hedge on your left and shortly reach the field corner and bear right. If you cannot easily locate this path you may prefer to use the following directions in parentheses. (With the church wall on your left go straight ahead

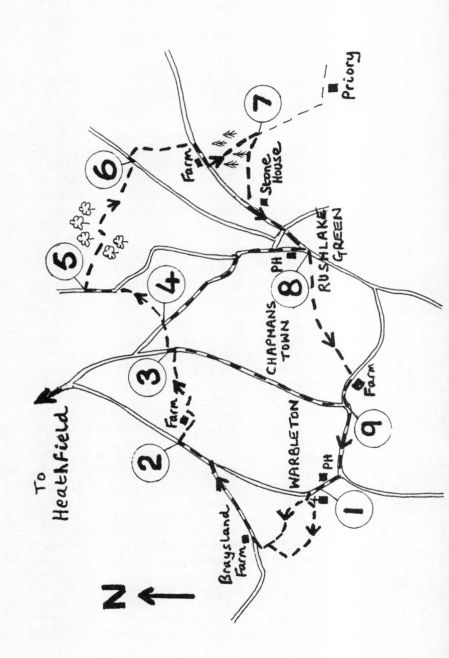

down the field and continue with a line of small trees on your left. Reach the field corner and bear right and, at the next corner, bear right again. Continue following the field edge which later turns left then right again.) In about 50 yards turn left, down a bank, into a lane opposite a white house (Braysland Farm). Turn right along the lane and in a little less than ½ mile reach a road and turn left along this for about 250 yards until you come to some corrugated iron buildings. There are good views over to Heathfield on your left.

2. Turn right on the gravelled drive to White Birch Farm. Go through a small iron gate and continue ahead. Go through the next gate, with the farmhouse over on your left, to reach the entrances to two fields. Take the left entrance, turning left and continuing into a second field. Turn right and follow the hedge, going over the barbed-wire fence ahead. Bear left down a bank, then cross a stream and go up to a stile leading you into a field. Continue along the right side of the field and after passing a large barn reach a lane.

**If you wish to take the 3 mile walk:** Turn right along the lane, which takes you through Chapman's Town, the site of an old windmill, and in less than a mile you reach a road and turn right. **Continue from point 9**.

3. Turn left along the lane and, in a few yards, turn right. Head diagonally left across a field (the path may be ploughed out). About 20 yards before the field corner go through an opening in the hedge and continue ahead on a path which runs alongside a garden and leads you out to a road.

**If you wish to take the 4 mile walk:** Turn right along the road, later passing a donkey and miniature pony farm. In a little less than a mile you will reach Rushlake Green. **Continue from point 8**.

4. Cross the road, go over a barrier and straight down a field (the path may be ploughed out) to reach some woods and a footbridge which you cross. Bear left across a field towards a barrier and onto a wide track. Go over another barrier and onto an enclosed footpath. You reach a lane on which you bear left and continue along for about 200 yards just past the last house on the right (Ghyllside).

5. Turn right through a metal gate and across a field and through another gate. Go down the left side of a field and over a stile leading you into a wood. In about 30 yards turn left over a ditch and shortly your path bears right, with a field over on your left, through some fallen trees and down to a plank bridge taking you over a stream. Bear left and where you reach a waymarked post continue ahead up a slope and reach a crossing track with

fingerposts. Follow the direction of the yellow waymark ahead, soon going over a barrier and alongside a plantation. Later the main path curves right but you go straight ahead, across the bracken, shortly reaching a barrier. Continue ahead across a field and over another barrier. Go over a stream and a further barrier. Proceed along the right side of a field to the next of these barriers. Cross the last field and go under a holly arch to a lane.

**6.** Turn left for a few yards to a public footpath sign on the right by a chapel. Climb a stile and continue past a small pond on your right. To the left of some old buildings you will find a broken stile which you cross and turn right. Pass a farmhouse on your right and, with a hedge on your right, continue to the bottom of a field. Go over a tall barrier and along the left side of the next field and reach a road. Turn right past Bunce's Farm and in about 200 yards turn left on a bridleway signposted to Sandbanks. Continue for about ¼ mile to pass the end of a wood on your right and, a few yards before a gate ahead, locate a stile by a gate on the right. (Continue ahead for another ½ mile if you wish to see the remains of the priory (HN).)

**7.** Turn right over the stile, doubling back a little, and continue along the edge of a field with the woods still on your right. Go through a gate and then bear right across another field making for a stile which is a little to the right of a line of oak trees. Bear left across the next field, passing some large tree stumps on your right, making for a house ahead, and go down a slope to a stile leading you out to a road. Bear left along the road and, after passing a large house on your left (Stone House) you go over a crossing road and reach Rushlake Green (HN). The Horse and Groom pub is on the opposite side. To continue the walk bear left and about 100 yards past the post office/village store you reach a telephone box.

**8.** Turn right through a kissing gate with a sad dedication and continue on a public footpath. You are led into woods, then over a footbridge followed by a stile. Proceed along the side of a field and over a stile by a gate. Bear right, following the direction of a fingerpost. Go over another stile and footbridge and along the right side of a field to yet another stile and bridge leading you into more woodland. Eventually you go through a barrier and onto a road opposite Kingley Hill Farm. Turn right along the road and shortly reach a right turn.

**9.** Follow the road signposted to Warbleton church which you will reach in another ½ mile. At the next road junction turn right to the pub and church.

## Historical Notes

**The War Bill-In-Tun Inn** may sound like a dreadful play on words. Its derivation is from the story of an impetuous soldier. Disliking the opening hours of the day, he used his halberd, or bill, to hack open a barrel, or tun.

**Warbleton church** has an unusual galleried manorial pew which is reached by climbing 12 steps. Since 1722 the privileged users have benefited from a commanding view of the chancel and pulpit. On the west wall of the nave a plaque tells the story of a local ironmaster, Richard Woodman, a churchwarden here in the 16th century. He immoderately accused the rector of changing his allegiance from Protestant to Catholic to suit the persuasion of the reigning monarch. The price he paid for his effrontery was to be burned at the stake in Lewes in 1557.

**Warbleton Priory**, dating from 1413 in Henry IV's reign, enjoys an isolated position. In later years it was converted into a farm but is now used as a hotel and restaurant. Ghastly goings-on in its history are indelibly recorded by bloodstains on one of the hotel's floors. There are two skulls preserved in the building and it is said that when any attempt is made to bury them ghostly wailings are heard in the night and local farmers complain that their stock goes sick.

**Rushlake Green** made its own rules for scoring boundaries at cricket. As the green does not offer a full size pitch, in 1903 it was decided that three runs would be awarded for a ball that bounced off the green, four runs for a hit that cleared it without bouncing and six for the mighty whack which took it over roofs of the surrounding cottages.

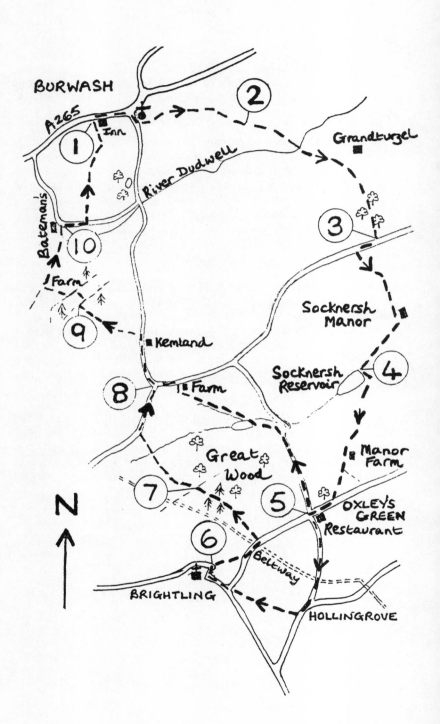

# Burwash
# and Brightling

**Introduction:** Here is Wealden country at its best and many of
the paths used offer excellent views across it. It is a particularly
pleasant walk which is undemanding and without any significant
climbs. The beginning of the walk takes you along almost the entire
length of the attractive village of Burwash and halfway round you
are led to another picturesque settlement at Brightling.

**Distance:** The full walk is about 8 miles but it is possible to reduce
this to around 6½ miles. It will take around 3½ hours or 3 hours
respectively.

**Refreshments:** There are three pubs in Burwash, all close to the
walk start. The historic Bear Inn is adjacent to the car park but
even more interesting, perhaps, is the Rose and Crown almost
opposite, and a little further along the main street is The Bell
which is also worth checking out. Besides the inns there is a tea
shop and also shops selling confectionery and ice cream. At the
point where you decide whether to complete the full walk or take
the shortened version you have The Fuller's Arms, a former pub,
now a restaurant. Bookings are advisable here (0424 82212).

**How to get there:** Burwash is on the A265 and is 6 miles east of
Heathfield. The walk commences from the free car park next to
the Bear Inn. Park towards the rear as the front section is reserved
for those parking for two hours or less. Buses run to Burwash from
Heathfield on Mondays to Fridays. On weekdays there is a service
to Brightling from Battle. OS maps 199 or 1270 (TQ 62/72), grid
reference TQ 673246.

**The Walk**
**1.** From the car park return to the road and turn right down the
main street passing a rather unusual ceramic map (HN) of the
village on your right. Cross the road by the war memorial (HN)
and enter the churchyard, passing the church (HN) on your left.

Pass some seats, leave the churchyard via a gate, then go down some stone steps and continue straight ahead, passing a seat. Go under the boughs of a mighty oak tree and over a stile into an area of parkland. Bear diagonally right downhill to a stile in a corner. In a few yards find another stile on your left and cross into a large field over which you continue slightly right towards a gate. Now bear diagonally right down a field to another gate. Bear left, still downhill, to pass some log horse jumps on your right and reach a pair of stiles.

**2.** Once over the stiles bear diagonally right across a field just clipping the corner of a small, fenced wood and go over a stile. Go straight across the next field towards a stile which you do not cross and turn right down the side of the field. Go over the next stile and continue along the edge of the next field. Cross the river Dudwell via a concrete bridge and go straight over the next field and uphill to a stile by a metal gate. Bear left across the next field and go through a wooden gate next to a metal one, then over a ditch. Bear right up a slope, with two white houses (Grandturzel and Little Grandturzel) over on your left, and go through a gate. Bear right onto a tarred driveway soon going through a gate by a cattle grid. Continue on the driveway under trees for almost $\frac{1}{2}$ mile and come out to a road.

**3.** Turn right along the road for about 200 yards and then turn left on the tarred driveway signposted to Socknersh Farm. After passing the gates leading to Socknersh Manor (HN) continue past a stone barn and then turn right. The tar soon runs out and you continue on the farm road for almost $\frac{1}{2}$ mile to reach Socknersh Reservoir (HN).

**4.** The farm road bears left and in a little over another $\frac{1}{2}$ mile you go through a gateway to reach Manor Farm. Immediately after passing a small pond on your right go up a slope to a stile. Bear left past a garden border to another stile and then bear left and right around a conifer plantation, passing a seat on your left. Go through a small metal gate and bear left past an old corrugated iron structure. Pass through some woods with a pond down on your right and another over on the left and go over a stile by a gate and out to a road. Turn right along the road and soon reach a crossroads at Oxley's Green with The Fuller's Arms on your left. **If you are doing the whole walk continue from point 5.**

**For the shorter walk continue as follows:** Turn right down the road signposted to Burwash and continue on it for about $\frac{1}{2}$ mile. Where the road turns sharply right leave it and continue straight ahead on a bridleway. Keep right at a fork and pass a reed-choked lake. You may hear the sound of rushing water on your right.

Continue with a stream over on your left and eventually climb up to a farmyard. Bear right past buildings out to a road. Turn left along the road and reach a junction. **Continue from point 8.**

**5. For the full 8 mile walk:** Turn left along the road and continue for about ½ mile passing under a bridge carrying a vulcanised beltway (HN) on your way. The road ascends to a junction in the settlement of Hollingrove. Turn right in the direction of Netherfield. Shortly turn right on a footpath by the entrance to Little Hollingrove Farm, soon bearing left onto an enclosed path. Go through a kissing gate and along the right side of a field with a water tower over on your left. When the hedge on your right curves left go through another kissing gate and straight across a field. A stile leads you into the next field and you continue ahead to a road. Cross the road and continue straight ahead towards the church in the village of Brightling (HN). The road curves right and soon left where there is a gravelled drive leading to some houses.

**6.** Turn sharp right on the drive and soon bear left through a small gate, then across a meadow and over a stile. Bear left down the side of the field and shortly bear right across it to a kissing gate and out to a road. Turn left along the road and, after going over the beltway that you went under earlier, turn immediately left into a field. Soon go over a stile into Great Wood, down some steps and bear right. Your path descends gently and may be boggy. Turn left over a stile and continue descending. A succession of yellow-topped posts confirm that you are still on the right track. Later go over a plank bridge and then a wide forestry track into a dark conifer plantation. You are led out of the woods via a stile to a crossing bridleway.

**7.** Go over the bridleway to another stile and enter an area of scrubland, still on a meandering path which is no longer waymarked – so take care! You are led down to another stile and over a brook. Continue straight up the side of a large field. There is no discernible path here but if you keep the woods immediately on your left you eventually reach a stile at the top of the slope leading you into the woods. Continue on an enclosed, brambly path and out to a road. Turn right along the road and in ¼ mile reach a junction.

**8.** Continue on the road signposted to Burwash and Bateman's and in another ¼ mile you reach a white-painted house called Kemland. Just past the house turn left into, and go straight across, a very large field. On the far side of the field go through a gate onto a wide track through trees and reach a T junction.

**9.** Turn right along a wide forestry road and in about 100 yards you will find a clear left turn. Go down through an area of fallen trees and reach a T junction by a footpath sign. Turn left and in about 200 yards find a gate on your right leading you into a field. Bear diagonally left to go through a gate next to a water trough. Bear left down to a stile and gate to the left of the barns of Park Farm. Once through the farmyard turn right on a track which takes you past an old mill house, back over the river Dudwell, and shortly you find Bateman's (HN) over on your left.

**10.** At the mansion turn right along a road and in another 200 yards or so go over a stile on your left by a concrete public footpath sign. Go up the right side of a field, then through an opening by the remains of a stile and up the next field with a wood and a pond on your left. Go straight up to a squeeze stile in a hedge and along the left edge of the next field. Go over the next stile and straight across the next field. Another stile and a plank bridge are crossed and you go sharp left up the side of the next field. Go over one more stile and you are led back into the car park.

### Historical Notes

**Burwash** has some interesting Georgian, as well as much older, architecture and is well worth exploring.

The ceramic map shows all the byways of the parish. In 1970 a local artist, Eileen Ware, was commissioned by the daughter of Judge Ellam and his wife to produce the work in their memory.

The war memorial includes the name of one Lieutenant John Kipling, the only son of the famous Rudyard. Aged just 18 he was posted missing after the Battle of Loos during the Great War of 1914–18. There are about 100 names commemorated on the memorial. On the anniversary of each death a light is switched on at the top of the memorial as a reminder of the loss.

The church presents a mystery. A cast-iron slab on its wall has some scarcely decipherable Lombardic lettering in memory of 'Jhnone Colins' which hints at a 14th century dating. However historians have proved that cast-iron did not come to Sussex until 1497 and that the material was not used for grave slabs until halfway through the following century.

**Socknersh Manor** is of individual design and an outstanding example of Tudor geometric brickwork. There is also a magnificent stone-built barn.

**Socknersh Reservoir** is particularly tranquil and attractive. It is one of many in the area that were artificially formed when the river Dudwell was dammed at several points to form hammer ponds.

The ensuing fast flow of water worked trip hammers crucial to the iron industry that prospered in the Sussex Weald from Roman times until the age of steam.

**The vulcanised beltway** runs in a figure of eight from Brightling Mine to Mountfield Mine. The continuous conveyor belt, which never stops moving, carries gypsum for a total of almost 8 miles.

**Brightling** was the home of 'Mad Jack' Fuller. He left his stamp on the village with a series of follies including the Temple, the Tower, the Sugar Loaf, the Pyramid and Brightling Needle. The 22-stone idiosyncratic local squire made his money from the Sussex iron trade. In order to get the local vicar to agree to the construction of a 25 ft mausoleum in his memory, some 24 years before his death, he arranged for the closure of the village pub, The Green Man. It was opposite the church and the vicar considered it to be a threat as some of his flock seemed to prefer drinking to attending church. 'Mad Jack' provided for another to be opened ½ mile down the road: The Fuller's Arms at Oxley's Green.

**Bateman's** was built in 1634 by John Brittan, a local ironmaster. It has been described as 'the loveliest small house in Sussex'. Now owned by the National Trust, it was the home of the district's most famous resident, Rudyard Kipling, from 1902 until his death in 1936 and is kept more or less as the writer left it. The mill, the woods and the streams that surround the house were the location for *Puck of Pook's Hill* which Kipling wrote in 1906 for his son and daughter. The stories reflect the local history and mythology of this charming part of Sussex.

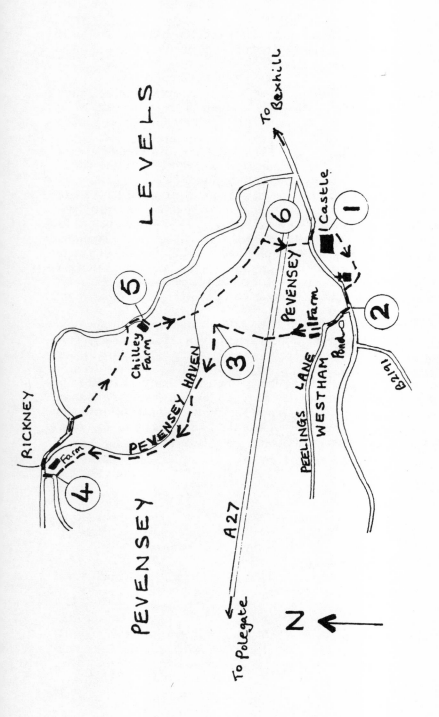

# Pevensey Castle and The Levels

**Introduction:** A pleasant, level walk over an area of former marsh-land drained for its rich fertility. It commences from Pevensey Castle which once protected the harbour but now lies a mile inland. If walking on your own you will enjoy almost complete solitude on this route, your only companions being the great variety of birds you would expect to find in an area so much dominated by water.

**Distance:** This circuit of almost 5 miles will take around 2–2¼ hours.

**Refreshments:** There are at least three public houses in Pevensey serving food all the year round and an equal number of tea shops, including one by the castle, open in the summer months.

**How to get there:** Pevensey is on the A259 between Eastbourne and Bexhill and just off the A27 running from Polegate. The walk commences from the car park by Pevensey Castle. Buses run from Eastbourne and Rye via Bexhill on Mondays to Fridays. Pevensey is served by trains on the Hastings–Eastbourne line. OS maps 199 or 1309 (TQ 60/70), grid reference TQ 646047.

**The Walk**

1. At the bottom of the car park go through a gate and bear right, passing Pevensey Castle (HN) on your right. Go over a concrete ford and onto an enclosed path towards Westham church (HN). Enter the churchyard through a gate, bear right past the church and out to a road. Cross the road, turn left and, just before a pedestrian crossing, reach a turning on the right (Peelings Lane).

2. Turn right passing the village hall on your right and pond on your left. Continue up the lane and reach the entrance to Castle Farm. Turn right and go through the farmyard, down past a pond and then over a field. Go through a farm gate in the hedge and continue on to reach a footbridge, stile and steps leading you over

the A27. Go down more steps to a stile and then across a field to a gateway. Bear slightly left towards a gap in the hedge and go across a ditch then over a stile by a barrier.

**3.** Turn left, soon ignoring a gate on your left. Follow a ditch on your left, go through a bridle gate and maintain direction across the next field. Go through a gap in a hedge and continue with a river, the Pevensey Haven, over on your right. Enter the next field over a bridge and leave it via a bridle gate next to a farm gate. Keep right, still close to the river, and go over another ditch where you may hear the sound of rushing water. Head towards an electricity pylon which you pass on your right, reach a fence in front of some farm buildings and go through a bridle gate on the left. Go through another gate and on past the farm buildings. You join a tarred drive and come out to a road at Rickney.

**4.** Turn right, over a bridge and, at a T junction with a signpost, turn right on the road going to Pevensey. Soon go over another bridge and continue along the road for about ¼ mile, as it turns left and left again. At the second turn you reach a gate on the right. Turn right here and in a few yards go through a gateway. Go straight across a field in a south-easterly direction towards a footbridge which you cross. Bear right towards a gate and continue ahead to go through the next one. Bear left and go through, or over, two more gates back to the road you left earlier. Turn right along the road for about 200 yards and reach the entrance to Chilley Farm.

**5.** Bear right on the farm track and, after passing some houses on your right, turn left through a gate and go diagonally right across a field and over a footbridge and stile. Maintain your south-easterly direction by bearing slightly right, soon going over a ditch (no bridge here) and reach a footbridge taking you back over the Pevensey Haven. Turn left and shortly go through a gap in a hedge passing a ditch on your right. Now bear right across a large, rough field with Pevensey Castle on the skyline ahead. You reach a gate by a bridleway/footpath sign and bear left. Shortly go through a farm gate by a sluice gate and continue ahead towards the next farm gate.

**6.** Do not go through the farm gate but turn right towards the A27 which you cross via gates. Join a track and come out to the road by the castle. Turn left and you will soon be back at the car park.

**Historical Notes**

**Pevensey** was the port chosen by William the Conqueror to land his powerful invasion fleet in 1066 and a castle was subsequently built here. The Romans had built the original fortress, named Anderida, and this was enlarged over the centuries to become the impressive building you see today with walls 12 ft thick and 10 ft high enclosing an area embracing almost 10 acres. Its chronicle covers the whole saga of English history. It was last reinforced in 1940 to help thwart the anticipated German invasion.

Opposite the castle, across the single street that runs through the village, stands the much-restored Old Mint House proving the area's one time importance as a hub of commerce. When it was no longer used for the minting of the coinage of the realm many interesting characters made it their home. One such was Andrew Borde, physician to Henry VIII, who with his rumbustious personality became known as 'Merry Andrew', a phrase that has stayed in common English usage to this day.

Pevensey Levels, which you traverse over much of the walk, was important for salt-making in medieval times. The area may look bleak and empty today but is a haven for wildlife and particularly interesting for bird watchers. Here were erected Martello Towers built to withstand another French invasion, that of Napoleon, in the early part of the last century. There were originally 74, extending from Folkestone to Seaford.

**Westham** is Pevensey's very close neighbour and struggles to retain its separate identity. Inside the church, the first to be built by the Normans after the Conquest, is a fragment of Solomon's temple. In 1860 the vicar, Howard Hopley, visited the newly-excavated foundations of the first Temple of Jerusalem and unashamedly broke off a lump. A communal grave in the churchyard, marked by four unpretentious stones, is the last resting place of the local victims of the 1666 plague.

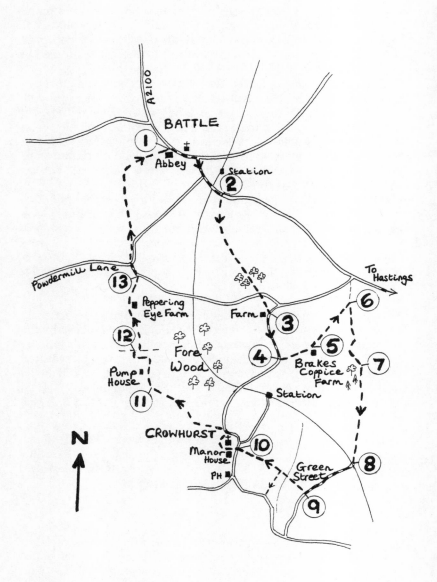

# Battle
# and Crowhurst

**Introduction:** It would be difficult to find anyone who had not heard of William the Conqueror, the Battle of Hastings and 1066 (and all that!). This walk commences in the shadow of Battle Abbey, founded by this legendary Norman warrior. It takes you on an attractive and reasonably level route via fields and farms to the other well-known East Sussex village of Crowhurst where you can see the ruins of its ancient manor house.

**Distance:** The approximately 7½ mile circuit will take you 3½ to 4 hours of steady walking.

**Refreshments:** Battle has several pubs, tea shops and other shops where confectionery, soft drinks and ice cream are on sale. A short diversion halfway round the walk will take you to The Plough Inn at Crowhurst.

**How to get there:** Battle, on the A2100, is 5 miles north west of Hastings. Besides the car park at Battle Abbey there are others in the town. The walk can also be commenced from point 10 in Crowhurst, there being a small parking area opposite the church and a larger one by the recreation ground. Battle and Crowhurst are well served by trains on the Tunbridge Wells–Hastings line. Buses run to Battle from Hastings, Eastbourne and Bexhill, Mondays to Saturdays, and to Crowhurst from Battle, Hastings and Bexhill, Mondays to Fridays. OS maps 199 or 1290 (TQ 61/71), grid reference TQ 748157.

### The Walk
**1.** Commence the walk by facing the gates of Battle Abbey (HN) and turning left on a raised pavement alongside the stone wall. You pass the Museum of Shops and church on your left and at The Chequers pub bear right down Lower Lake. Go over Powdermill Lane and pass The Senlac Hotel, then a road leading to the station on your left and a filling station on the right.

**2.** Opposite St. Mary's Terrace turn right on a roadway, soon joining an enclosed path. Shortly the views on your right open out and you go over a stile and maintain direction along a rough field. At a fork keep left, go over a crossing track and then a stile onto an enclosed path through woods. Continue across a field, initially following a line of poles, and reach the corner. Go downhill through woods, over a stream and then over a stile. Climb steeply straight across the next field and go over a stile at the end of a row of trees. Cross over a lane and go up a bank to another stile leading you into a field. Follow the wire fence on your left and reach the white gates leading into Wheatcroft Farm.

**3.** Turn right on a road and shortly pass the Crowhurst village sign. You will be taken to the village centre but on a less direct route. The road curves left as you pass the entrance to Wheatcroft Rural Workshops and you continue along the road past Blacklands Farm shop and Pye's Farm. You may wish to change sides to be on the outside of the road bends in order to increase the visibility of any oncoming traffic. Where the road curves right you reach the entrance to Brakes Coppice Farm park.

**4.** Turn left through the white gates and continue on the tarred track. At a junction of tracks go straight ahead, still on the tar, downhill and soon up again. Look for a path on the right through trees, cutting a corner of the drive, reach the tar again and bear right, still uphill towards the farmhouse.

**5.** Just before a farm gate turn left over a stile which leads to two more, to avoid going through the farmyard. You come onto the farm track and go over yet another stile, by a gate, and are led past some corrugated iron buildings. Remain on this track for almost another ½ mile, with a valley down on your right and the coastline in view towards the horizon. As you pass under power lines look back and take in the panoramic view. The track bears left and you find a stile on the right.

**6.** Cross the stile and bear right down the side of a field, later crossing a narrow line of shrubs, still bearing right to go through a farm gate by some old buildings. Pass a white house on your right and continue ahead on a farm track. The track climbs a slope and as it levels out, about 50 yards before a farm gate, bear right across the field to a white-painted stile in the fence.

**7.** Continue ahead into woods on a winding, tree-strewn path and eventually reach a stile. You may find some conveniently fallen trees here serving as seats if you are ready for a rest. Once over the stile bear right along a field edge following a fence as it turns left and then right. Join a wide farm track continuing on this for ¼ mile where you go through a farm gate and over a crossing track. Continue ahead and gradually descend towards trees. Later another track comes in from the right and in a few minutes you reach a lane at Stone Bridge Cottage.

**8.** Bear right over a railway bridge on Swainham Lane. Continue for almost ½ mile through the settlement of Green Street, passing a converted oast house (Green Acres Oast), and immediately find the entrance to Oldfields and a concrete footpath sign.

**9.** Turn right onto the footpath and soon go over a stile and then another. Turn right onto a potentially overgrown and muddy track – you may find a mud-avoidance path on the left for part of the way. Go over a stile by a brick wall and turn left, the mud now giving way to brambles, and you soon go over a bridge across a dismantled railway. Skirt a large, fallen tree on your right and go over a stile leading to a farm track. (If you wish to visit The Plough, turn left down the track to a road on which turn right. The pub is at a road junction and from there you should continue along the road to reach point 10.) Cross over to the stile opposite, go through some brambles, and out to a field. If you find the field ploughed or in crop and the path indiscernible you may prefer to turn left and continue around the field edge until you reach a farm gate close to the corner. A right of way exists as follows: bear diagonally right across the field, passing some trees and a dried up pond on your right. Continue across with Crowhurst church ahead in the distance and reach a farm gate on the left close to the corner of the field. Go through the gate and bear right down a slope to cross a bridge and gate. Proceed along the right side of a field, pass through a farmyard. A gate leads you out to a road almost opposite St. George's church in Crowhurst (HN).

**10.** Cross the road to the track opposite and, in a few yards, reach the ruins of the manor house, thought to date from the 12th century. Retrace your steps and turn left into the churchyard and follow the path, passing the church on your right, and come out to a road. Turn left along the road and, where it curves right, turn left onto a grassy footpath along a field with the backs of houses on your right. Maintain direction across the field to a stile leading you onto a narrow, brambly path. Go through a gate and bear slightly right across the next field to a stile leading you into Fore Wood Nature Reserve. Continue straight ahead down to a pond where you turn left. Pass a couple of turnings on the right and at a fork, by a bench, bear left along the edge of the wood. Later your path bears left over a plank bridge.

**11.** Turn right along a field with a stream on your right and continue into the next field. Pass an enclosed copse containing a brick pumping house on your left and when you come to a bridge turn sharp left across the field. You reach a tarred farm track and turn right through a gate, then uphill to a T junction by Powdermill Cottage.

**12.** Turn right and soon go over a bridge by a waterfall. Continue on a driveway past the strangely-named Peppering Eye Farmhouse and eventually come out to a road.

**13.** Turn left and soon reach a road junction. Cross over Powdermill Lane and go up a bank to a footpath which runs parallel to the road below on the right. You reach a crossing farm track where you go over a stile, past farm buildings and over another stile by a gate. Go down the side of a field, over the next stile by a gate and past a spinney. Maintain direction along the next field, over a stile and uphill. Another path joins from the left and now on your right you find the wire fence, enclosing the grounds of Battle Abbey, which you follow. Go through a gate and bear right back into Battle.

**Historical Notes**

**Battle Abbey**, whose large 14th century gates face the main square, was built shortly after 1066, its altar identifying the site where King Harold fell. The ruins are open to visitors during the summer. The square was once the village green and located here is a brass plate marking the place where bulls were tethered – the town having a well-known association with the 'sport' of bull-baiting. Although many of the buildings in this small town have their roots in medieval times their frontages are more recent 18th and 19th century additions. The cottages close to the abbey are 17th century but just beyond the gatehouse is a well-preserved example of medieval, timber-framed architecture which was once a welcome haven for pilgrims visiting the locality.

At the end of the walk, as you return to the town, the enclosed area on your right is the site where the 7,000-strong Norman army formed up in preparation for their defeat of the English.

**Crowhurst** churchyard has a venerable yew estimated to be anything from a youthful 1000 years to an awe-inspiring 3000 years. Is this a record? The tree, so ravaged over time that one or two grown men can climb inside, must have been there when William's army rode by.

# Hastings and Fairlight Country Park

**Introduction:** A fairly energetic, coastal walk, with outstanding views, commencing from Fairlight, 2½ miles east of Hastings. You pass several beauty spots as you are taken over sandstone cliffs and through quiet glens. Towards the end of the walk Firehills, so named because of its blaze of gorse, provides an added attraction in spring. There is the chance to visit a secluded cove which is sandy at low tide and a fine site for a picnic.

**Distance:** The full walk is about 6 miles but this may be reduced by about 1½ miles. The complete circuit, which has many climbs, requires around 2¼–2½ hours. A diversion of only a couple of hundred yards will take you down to the sandy, rocky cove.

**Refreshments:** Refreshment facilities are provided by the lower car park during summer months and there is a tea shop near the top car park. Early on in the walk (point 2) you may find the tea shop at Fairlight Place is open. For something stronger you will need to travel down the road to the Fairlight Lodge Hotel or into Hastings itself.

**How to get there:** 2½ miles east of Hastings, leave Fairlight Road at the entrance to Fairlight Country Park and in about 100 yards reach and use the first car park on the left. Alternatively, walk along the coast from Hastings Old Town and commence at point 4. There is an infrequent bus service from Hastings to Fairlight. OS maps 199 or 1291 (TQ 81/91), grid reference TQ 860115.

**The Walk**
**1.** From the Fairlight Country Park (HN) car park go down the road to the Visitor Centre and another car park, passing a memorial to Grey Owl (HN). Continue along a lane towards coastguard cottages but, just before reaching them, turn right over a stile and go across a field to a gate. Bear right on a wide, grassy track and eventually pass a derelict house on your left. Go over a stile and

87

TO HASTINGS

FAIRLIGHT ROAD  FAIRLIGHT

VISITOR CENTRE

FIRE HILLS

① ⑥ ⑦

FAIRLIGHT PLACE

② ③ ④ ⑤

COVEHURST BAY

ECCLESBOURNE RESERVOIR

N

across a field. You reach a junction of paths, cross a stile and go ahead with a fence on your right. Continue over a series of stiles with fields on your right until you reach the entrance to Fairlight Place.

**2.** Proceed on a tarred lane for about ½ mile, ignoring turnings left and right and passing a pair of houses. After passing a wooden barn over on your left you reach a gate.

**3.** Turn left on a farm drive and, in a few yards, go over a stile by a gate and continue downhill. Soon go through woods and bear left with the track, passing a waterfall. You reach a fork at post 6 and continue ahead in the direction of Ecclesbourne Glen reaching another fork. Keep right, downhill, and shortly pass Ecclesbourne Reservoir on your right. You reach an open area at post 5 and bear left in the direction of Ecclesbourne Glen. Ignore a turning on the right and continue uphill on a wide, grassy track. You reach post 4 and continue straight ahead with a fence on your left and come to a T junction.

**4.** Turn left, at first between fences, and later you start to climb with the fence now only on your right and notices indicating dangerous cliffs beyond. Just before a left turn you go through an opening in the fence and then through some small trees. Continue on a wide track, later passing a wooden seat. Pass a turning on the left and post 7 to continue ahead downhill in the direction of Fairlight Glen. Soon go down some steps with a useful handrail, past a seat and post 8. Continue downhill on a wide, grassy track. Ignore a narrow right turn and reach a junction of paths at post 10. Turn right and shortly cross a stream.

**5.** (If you wish to visit the secluded bay, sandy at low tide, turn right down into Fairlight Glen. A flight of steps will lead you safely down the steep slope into the bay. Retrace your steps to the main track.)

Continue uphill along the coastal track and reach post 11 where you turn right up some steps. Later pass post 12 and soon descend some steps. At a junction of paths by post 13 go straight ahead, descending quite steeply. Pass a seat, go over a stream and start climbing again, gently at first and later more steeply where you are assisted by some steps. You reach a bench (Lovers' Seat – HN) and turn right, soon ascending once more and later you will find yourself below the coastguard station at post 14.

**6. To shorten the walk by about 1½ miles:** Turn left uphill past the coastguard station and cottages back up the road to the car park.

**To continue with the full walk:** Go ahead bearing right on a wide, grassy track above the cliffs. Where the path divides keep to the right, still hugging the cliff top. You reach some houses at Fairlight Cove and a sign board at post 17.

**7.** Turn left uphill, keeping left at a fork, bearing left on a fine hilltop path and eventually reach a plank seat at post 15. With the seat on your right continue ahead towards the coastguard station. Go through a metal barrier and turn right back to the car park.

**Historical Notes**

**Fairlight Country Park** is an extremely attractive area with unspoilt sandstone cliffs divided by vigorous streams rushing down to the sea. There are good views to the east towards Rye and the Romney Marshes beyond and, on a clear day, the coast of France may be glimpsed.

Several ships have foundered in this vicinity including one, in the last century, that spilled bodies, fragments of pianofortes and casks of brandy on the shore. The locals rushed to the scene and, having no one to save, some drank themselves to death, lying amongst the corpses.

This was also an area where 'owling', or illegal exporting, was rife. Two centuries ago the law forbade the export of wool, other than in a manufactured form. Although fines were heavy for those caught, 'owlers' were prepared to take the risks for the lucrative rewards they reaped.

**Grey Owl**, otherwise Archie Belaney, attended Hastings Grammar School and, infatuated with all things Indian, in his teens he emigrated to Canada and became an expert trapper, literally 'going native'. He returned to England in the 1930s giving lectures and publicising his books on wildlife and the natural relationship between man and wild animals.

**Lovers' Seat** was once a large sandstone outcrop on the cliff edge which fell into the sea many years ago. Folklore has it that it was on this rock that two lovers regularly met. When one left by boat from the bay below rough seas swept its occupant away. The other lover attempted a rescue and jumped into the sea only to be similarly lost beneath the waves.

# Rye and Iden

**Introduction:** Starting from Rye, one of the most attractive and historic towns in East Sussex, this fairly gentle ramble should not use up too much of your time and energy, leaving you with plenty more to thoroughly explore the delightful town afterwards. You will discover some of the county's most scenic countryside with wide ranging views back over the town and across the Kent border towards the Romney Marshes. The route concludes with a pleasant stretch of river walking as the town's skyline becomes invitingly closer.

**Distance:** This approximately 8 mile walk will take about $3^{1}/_{4}$–$3^{1}/_{2}$ hours.

**Refreshments:** In Rye you have plenty of choice for refreshments, from pubs to restaurants, tea shops and, being close to a harbour, fish and chip shops, of course. Part way round the walk you have The Hare and Hounds at Rye Foreign and then The Bell at Iden. Also in Iden you have the post office/village stores where confectionery and ice cream are available six days a week.

**How to get there:** The walk commences from Rye station. Trains run hourly from Hastings and Ashford, Monday to Saturday, and two-hourly on Sundays. There is a bus service from Eastbourne via Battle on Mondays to Fridays and others from Hastings and Folkestone on Mondays to Saturdays. Services from surrounding villages are on a once-a-week basis. There are plenty of car parks to be found in the town. OS maps 189 or 1271 (TQ 82/92), grid reference TQ 919205.

**The Walk**

**1.** Facing the station turn left along the pavement and go over a level-crossing on the right. Bear right onto a footpath between a school and the Queen Adelaide pub. This path becomes raised and later you see the river Tillingham over on your left. Reach a stile on the left which you cross and continue on a raised

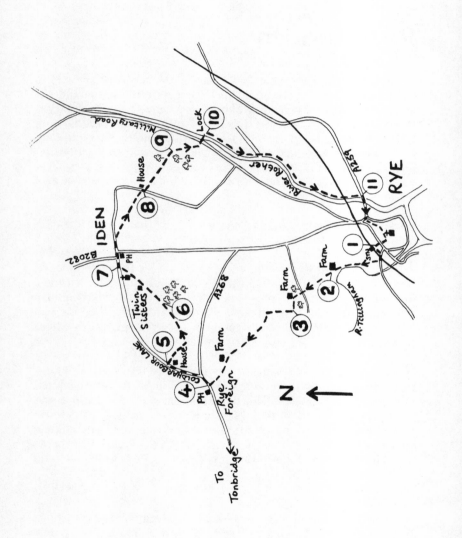

embankment which soon bears right. Cross another stile in front of a farmhouse.

**2.** Bear left through a gate and straight uphill across a field aiming for a stile on the skyline and to the left of some trees. After crossing the stile continue along a field with a fence on your right and through a kissing gate to a lane. Cross the lane and go over the stile opposite, then through a snatch of woodland and out to a farm road on which you bear left, and then left again, to reach an oast house and stables.

**3.** Turn right on a track which becomes sunken, and shortly ignore a left fork. Keep left at the next fork and where the track curves left go over a waymarked stile. Go down the left side of a field for about 100 yards where you cross a ditch on your left. Immediately turn right and go over another ditch, maintaining your original direction down the right side of the adjacent field to the bottom. Cross a stile and turn right then left along the edge of a field on a wide, grassy path. Cross a stile by a wide water channel and continue straight across the next field. Go over a bridge, through a gate and straight up the next field. Go through a gate and bear left onto a farm track. Once through the next gate bear left then right through a farmyard, with a pond on your right, and reach a road at Rye Foreign (HN). The Hare and Hounds is just across the road with an interesting house opposite.

**4.** Turn right along the road and shortly, at a junction, turn left on Coldharbour Lane signposted to Iden. Pass a white house (Coldharbour) and reach the end of its garden fence.

**5.** Turn right over a plank bridge and stile and continue along the edge of a field following a fence on your right which soon turns left. Soon you cross a stile and then bear left over a field with buildings on your right. In the field corner cross a stile, then turn right and immediately left along the side of a field with a fence on your right. You reach a large tree stump and bear diagonally left across the field. You should find and continue ahead on a wide, grassy track, aiming for the corner of a wood where you cross a stile by a brook.

**6.** Bear left then right round a field edge. Immediately after passing a pond on your left bear left then right again round the next field edge. Cross a stile to the right of a large house, Twin Sisters (HN), and continue along the next field to cross another stile passing a cottage and a pond. Continue straight across a recreation ground towards Iden church (HN). Enter the churchyard, passing the church on your left, and leave via a gate taking you out to a road in the village of Iden (HN).

**7.** Turn right along the road, soon passing the post office/village stores, and reach The Bell Inn. Cross the road to the turning opposite signposted to Houghton Green and Appledore. After passing the third bungalow on the right, turn right at a public footpath sign onto an enclosed path. Enter a large field via a stile, bear diagonally left and cross a stile in the fence. Go straight across the next field to its far corner, through a gateway and then bear left along the side of a field. You reach a stile which you do not cross but turn right and then left along the field edge with a pond on your left. Cross a stile and bear right over a large meadow towards a house. Go through a gate out to a lane.

**8.** Turn right for a few yards and, at the end of a garden fence, turn left over a stile and go along the left side of a field. In about 100 yards cross a stile on the left into the adjacent field and turn right to maintain your original direction. Turn right then left with the field edge, go through an opening by some water troughs and straight across the next field. Cross a stile leading into a wood. Go over a plank bridge, then over a stream (no bridge), shortly passing a footpath sign and bear left to cross a stile.

**9.** Bear diagonally right across a large field towards the end of a line of trees. Bear right over a stile and then bear left across a large field. Keep well to the left of two isolated trees and, about 50 yards after going under power lines, go over a stile in the fence on the left. Proceed with care down a stepped path (slippery after rain), later with the aid of a hand rail. Cross a footbridge and the Military Road (HN) and then cross the river Rother via Scots' Float Sluice.

**10.** Turn right over a stile and continue on a raised path along the river bank. Besides forming part of the Sussex Border Path this is also part of the Saxon Shore Way. Go over a stile and then over another by a sluice at the end of a water channel. Continue over three more stiles and, when you reach a railway bridge, go down the bank onto a path which avoids the mud and takes you across a stile under the bridge (watch your head). Scramble up the bank and continue on the raised path to reach the A259.

**11.** Turn right across the river into Rye (HN) and turn right at a roundabout. Shortly cross the road onto an enclosed path at the side of The Queen's Head pub. You reach a road and turn left, shortly going through Landgate (HN). Continue along Hilders Cliff and down on the left you will see the Town Salts (HN) and Romney Marshes way beyond. Proceed into Mint Street and the High Street. The second turning on the left is Lion Street. Look up to the top of the street here and you will see St. Mary's church (HN). On your right is the 17th century Old Grammar School.

Turn right down Market Road, across Cinque Ports Street, passing the Cinque Ports Inn, and you are back at the station.

## Historical Notes

**Rye Foreign** is said to derive its name from the fact that Huguenots fleeing from France to Rye formed a community here. Opposite the hamlet's pub is a most unusual thatched-roof building, its walls made of logs set end on, Cordbat Cottage. In the dialect of old Sussex a cordbat was a pile of logs.

**Twin Sisters** was at one time, as the name suggests, two houses. They were built as a present by a local rector for his twin granddaughters.

**Iden church**, dating from the 12th century, had only two incumbents in the 117 years from 1807 to 1924. Of interest to botanists is its belltower where maidenhair fern, usually only found on West Country cliffs, grows at the foot of the inside wall.

**Iden** once had its own 'castle', a castellated house surrounded by a moat, built in 1284. Unfortunately, all that remains of the castle, said at one time to rival Bodiam in its grandeur, is the moat and a remnant of the gateway.

**The Military Road** was built to service the Royal Military Canal, created to thwart the anticipated Napoleonic invasion. The Scots' Float Sluice was rebuilt in the 1980s but a small section of the brickwork survives from the time of the original building. In 1830 townspeople rioted claiming that it impeded the tidal flow up the estuary, critical to fishermen and bargees. The turmoil lasted two full days and nights until soldiers aimed their muskets and the mob dispersed.

**Rye** is a captivating, medieval 'time warp' with its narrow, cobbled streets where half-timbered houses jut over the pavements, mixed in with Georgian neighbours. In the 12th century Rye joined the Cinque Ports, becoming responsible for coastal defences against the French. In the 16th century the sea, which had previously lapped its shores, receded and left the town bounded only by the various river waters. These merge at the town and then flow 2 miles down to Rye harbour, now a separate village and a mile from the sea at low tide.

**The Landgate** is the sole survivor of Rye's four original gateways. Built in the early 14th century and enlarged and strengthened after the French sacked the town in 1377, it still has the grooves for its portcullis visible beneath the archway. The clock was installed in 1863 as a memorial to Prince Albert.

**The Town Salts**, a flat expanse of mown grass now used for recreation, was formerly the source of the town's salt supply. A shallow covering of seawater was permitted to flood the meadow. When the water evaporated the salt deposits were collected and used to preserve fish. Rye's greatly reduced fishing fleet moors nearby.

**St. Mary's church**, dating from the 12th century, has a splendid blue-and-cream clock in the tower. The gilded 'quarter boys' are replicas of the 1761 originals which can be seen inside the church.